THE PLOTS TO
KILL
HITLER

THE PLOTS TO
KILL
HITLER

THE MEN AND WOMEN WHO
TRIED TO CHANGE
HISTORY

RICHARD DARGIE

Picture Credits

Getty Images: 8, 17, 23, 35, 69, 76, 86, 89, 91, 94, 109, 116, 119, 133, 139, 163, 173

Shutterstock: 18, 31, 41, 45, 59, 66, 188

ED Archive: 55

Alamy: 63, 99

This edition published in 2019 by Arcturus Publishing Limited
26/27 Bickels Yard, 151–153 Bermondsey Street,
London SE1 3HA

AD006866UK

Printed in the UK

Contents

Introduction

O n 16 August 1914, Adolf Hitler enlisted in the 16th Bavarian Reserve Infantry Regiment. His mobilization papers came through on 7 October. After several weeks of basic training in southern Germany, Hitler and his new comrades arrived on the Western Front and were instantly thrown into the First Battle of Ypres. By the end of November, the 16th had lost more than 2,500 men killed or badly wounded. Only 700 men were left from its original strength of 3,300. One of the lucky few was Hitler, who noted that his 250-strong company had been reduced to 42 men after little more than a month of modern warfare. While so many around him had died in their first taste of combat, he had avoided death and maiming. It was around then that he began to believe he was a 'born survivor'.

A history of close calls

Over the next four years Hitler was present at many of the bloodiest actions on the Western Front as a front line soldier and later as a runner carrying messages to and from regimental HQ. He had two 'close shaves' that he considered miraculous. On 11 February 1915, an Allied 15 cm (6 in) shell landed directly on 'his' dugout. The shelter was destroyed, but there were no casualties and an unscathed Hitler was able to climb out of the mud and debris. On 25 September that same year he was eating at the Front with several comrades when, he later claimed, an inner voice told him to move away and stand further down the trench. Seconds later a shell burst above the point where Hitler had been sitting. All of his dinner companions were wiped out. Most soldiers would have put

Adolf Hitler in his field uniform during the First World War, around 1915.

their survival down to luck, chance or the random fortunes of war. For Adolf Hitler, however, it was clear evidence to him at least that he was being preserved for a purpose. He later remembered those incidents during the war years as the point in his life when he conquered the fear of death: the will to survive was now his 'undisputed master. Now Fate could bring on the ultimate tests without my nerves shattering or my reason failing.'

This inner fearlessness explains Hitler's reckless attitude to his own personal safety when he was embroiled in vicious political street fighting in the early 1920s. He delighted in using physical force to subdue his opponents. In the beer halls of Munich, he openly confronted his rivals at public meetings that often ended up in bloody brawling. He was the first European politician to take to the skies at a point in aviation history when flying was still an exceptionally dangerous way to travel. His lightning dashes around Germany in the fastest cars available to him were soon part of 'the Hitler legend'. Some thought him brave, many thought him foolhardy. He undoubtedly enjoyed a generous slice of luck, especially when it came to avoiding the many enemies who wanted to eliminate him.

A special protection

Many different kinds of people tried to kill Hitler. Some plotters were political opponents on the Left while others were Nazis who had grown unhappy with his leadership. Some would-be assassins were simply moral men and women who believed that Hitler and his politics were evil. In the last years of the Third Reich, most of those who tried to liquidate him were German patriots who believed he was dragging their country down to destruction. Hitler himself knew that if his enemies were determined enough they would get past all the security guards in the Reich and kill him. He would eventually surround himself with as many guards as any other dictator in history, yet he always trusted in his deep intuitive feeling that he was under some special protection that he called *Vorsehung* or Providence. His immense self-belief helps to explain the casual, nonchalant attitude that he sometimes took towards his own security, particularly when he was amongst his 'own people' in his adopted homeland of Bavaria. It also helps explain the serious risks that he took on the Eastern Front in the Second World War, undertaking many hazardous flights to front-line positions: at least one Soviet fighter pilot put bullets into his Condor.

This book recounts many of the plans to kill Hitler and the attempts by plotters to puncture his sense of invincibility. In doing so it provides an insight into the continual wariness, suspicion and cunning that were key elements of his character and essential for his self-preservation. It describes the many instances of chance, and sometimes farce, that thwarted plotters and saved the Führer for another day. It also explores the historical context of each of these plots in order to help explain how one of the most ruthless and hated dictators in history survived for so long and was ultimately able to choose his own moment to depart from a world that he had plunged into war and chaos.

CHAPTER 1

4 November 1921
The Beer Hall Assassin

The hall was packed. About 800 men had crowded into the Festsaal or ceremonial room on the upper floor of the Hofbräuhaus. The speaker that night was at the far end of the long barrel-vaulted room, standing alone on a large wooden beer table that jutted out towards the audience. He wore a black jacket and black tie and sported a short, clipped moustache. After he had been speaking for a few minutes, a man in the middle of the hall stood up and climbed on to his chair. He was wearing the clothes of a factory worker. Looking at the expectant faces of the men sitting around him, he could see that they were mostly working men like him. To a man, they were socialists and communists. They had not come to listen to the speaker that night but to put an end to his political career. The worker shouted out one word – *Freiheit*! Freedom. It was the signal for a huge roar to emerge from the throats of the angry men in the crowd. They were fuelled up for a fight. Each man had already added several litres of beer to the well of aggression within himself. They had stored their empty beer mugs under their chairs and now they subjected their enemy to a volley of heavy glass and stoneware missiles, flung at speed and powered by hate. Adolf Hitler later likened that moment to coming under fire from a volley of howitzer shells in the trenches of the Great War. Once the artillery bombardment was over, many of the workers began to open their knapsacks and remove their close combat weapons: lengths of metal pipe and brass knuckledusters. Their more lightly armed comrades brandished broken chair-legs. Hitler and his supporters had walked into an ambush and were completely outnumbered.

Socialist and communist organizers had secretly packed the hall with workers from three large factories in Munich: Kustermann's iron and steel foundry, the Maffei locomotive engineering plant and the Isaria electrical meter works. A telephone message meant to warn Hitler had arrived too late, a mess-up caused by the fact that the Nazi Party had moved into new headquarters that very day and its office still lacked a phone. Some stormtroopers had rushed to the Hofbräuhaus to rescue their leader, only to find that a thick cordon of police was letting no one enter the overcrowded hall. Hitler had recognized the danger he faced as soon as he arrived. He scanned the massed ranks of his opponents, who were 'stabbing him with their very eyes'. Remembering that night three years later in his book *Mein Kampf*, he described 'the innumerable faces turned towards me with sullen hatred', faces that were threatening to 'make an end of us and stop up our mouths for good'.

The battle of the beer hall

In his written version of the events that followed, Hitler transformed a beer hall brawl, common enough in a city bedevilled by political violence, into a moment of noble heroism. His telling of the punch-up deliberately echoed the tale of the 300 Spartans at the battle of Thermopylae. Hitler ordered the few men he had with him in the hall, perhaps 45 or so at most, to line up in soldierly order and he then gave them what he later regarded as the true founding speech of the Hitler movement. This was their chance to prove their loyalty, both to him and to their National Socialist beliefs. Whatever happened, he would remain in the hall until the last.

If any of them chose to desert the field of battle, he would personally tear off the dishonoured swastika insignia from that man's arm. But, said the future Führer, he did not believe that a single man there would prove to be a coward. And he assured his assembled troop: 'Not a man of us must leave this hall unless we are carried out dead.' When the brawl began, Hitler's men broke into platoons of ten or twelve and launched themselves against the vastly superior foe, 'attacking like wolves'. Not one of his men emerged from the fray without being covered in blood and badly scarred. Hitler later picked out his chauffeur Emil Maurice and his secretary Rudolf Hess for acts of conspicuous gallantry, or perhaps savagery.

According to Hitler's account of the events of that night, the riot continued for 20 minutes until the hellish noises of pitched battle and the howling of badly damaged men were silenced by two sharp cracks. Someone in the crowd had fired a gun, a would-be assassin who had planned to shoot Hitler. He had cleaned and loaded a pistol and carried it to the meeting in his coat pocket. Then he had sat drinking in the hall with his comrades while he listened to Hitler's opening remarks, waiting for the moment to shoot and kill the fascist madman. In the melee, his shots missed their target. In years to come, Nazi veterans of the Battle of the Hofbräuhaus would embellish their tale, as many old soldiers often do. They would remember their leader standing firm, taking out his gun and returning the fire of the assassin. Hitler certainly carried a gun on a daily basis at this point in his life, but in his memoir he made no mention of using it that night. He contented himself with praising his 'bleeding boys', who had routed the enemy and chased them from a hall that now looked as 'if a shell had struck it'. As they gathered themselves to have their dripping blood stopped and their wounds bandaged, the great Austrian orator rewarded his troops by climbing back up on to the wooden table and delivering the last 20 minutes of his interrupted speech.

The target

In 1921, Adolf Hitler became a target. It was the year that he first emerged as a significant figure in the explosive politics of Weimar Germany. On 3 February that year he spoke to over 6,500 people in the huge permanent hall of Munich's famous Circus Krone. National Socialists, identified by their red and white armbands bearing the still unfamiliar black *Hakenkreuz* (swastika), stood at the doors to the vast arena. They collected the entry fee of one mark from all who had come to hear the dynamic orator who was making a name for himself throughout southern Germany. Veterans of the First World War, students and the unemployed were allowed to enter without payment, but large posters by the doors warned Jews that they were not welcome and would not be admitted. A surging wall of fervent supporters pressed towards Hitler as he made his way to the podium and when he stepped forward on to the platform to begin to talk he was met with a euphoric reception from the gathered mass in front of him. It was the largest audience he had addressed in his brief political career. The flow of his speech was repeatedly interrupted by waves of applause and emotional outbursts of support. As he uttered his final word of the night, the crowd spontaneously burst into the popular *Deutschland Über Alles*, a song that was soon to become the German national anthem.

In *Mein Kampf*, Hitler later remembered the special importance of that night in February 1921. His success that evening, and at two further mass rallies at the Circus Krone later that month, signalled a key moment in German history when 'we could no longer be ignored'. On 29 July 1921 Hitler became chairman of the National Socialist German Workers' Party. With some deft manoeuvring, he sidelined its original founders and established his full control over the Nazi movement. That evening his followers addressed him for the first time as *unser Führer*, our Leader. Thanks to his personal dynamism, his organizational drive, his eloquence and a message that was attuned to the despair of the times, the Party membership was rising quickly. New branches were opening across Bavaria in the larger commercial towns such as Rosenheim and Augsburg. He had begun to attract wealthy right-wing donors in Berlin and their support helped put the Party newspaper *Völkischer Beobachter*, or People's Observer, on a sound financial footing.

By October he had made over 30 major speeches throughout southern Germany, usually electrifying his audience. In every one of these speeches he made it clear that he was in politics to crush and wipe away the internal enemies that had laid Germany low: the Jews, the communists, the bourgeois democratic parties of the Weimar Republic and the 'November Criminals' who had signed the shameful Armistice and Versailles Peace Settlement. He also made it clear from the outset that his methods would not be democratic or even legal. His enemies got the message and fought back. The level of violence at Nazi meetings rose. During the autumn of 1921, his opponents prepared for a decisive clash with Hitler in the Hofbräuhaus. They chose to attack on 4 November. That was the night when the NSDAP, the National Socialist German Workers' Party, was truly born in a violent clash of blood and brutality.

The fields of battle

Throughout its history, Munich was famous for its breweries and its many hostelries, beer cellars and beer gardens. For almost 500 years they had catered to the countless merchants and dozens of armies that passed through the city en route to Austria and Italy. In the late 1800s, Munich rapidly industrialized and its population soared. The larger breweries cashed in by building vast drinking halls which offered beer, food and entertainment to the city's growing number of residents. In the troubled years after the First World War, these halls became political pressure points in the struggle between Left and Right. Hitler's first major political speech was delivered in the Hofbräukeller in October 1919, to around 130 listeners. He was encouraged: most previous Party meetings had been attended by a mere handful of committee members.

Hitler quickly realized that the beer hall was a place where he could use his skills to project his furious polemic and attract new members to his political movement. He also understood that in the halls he could jeer, heckle, intimidate and even assault his political opponents when they were trying to speak. An ex-soldier, he had no qualms whatsoever about using physical violence as a political weapon. There was nothing unusual about that in post-war Germany. Riots and street brawls were common, as were political assassinations. There were at least 354 political killings in Germany between 1919 and 1922 and one right-wing group, Operation Consul, specialized in such murders. Two of its members murdered Matthias Erzberger, a Catholic Centre Party politician who had the bad luck to be sent to France in late 1918, in order to negotiate and ultimately sign the Armistice with the Allies in the Forest of Compiègne on 11 November. As a result, he became one of the defeatist 'November Criminals' whom Hitler despised as traitors. On 3 May 1921, Hitler demanded that Erzberger be arrested and tried for treason if he ever set foot in Bavaria. Later that summer, Erzberger was gunned down while on a family walking holiday in the Black Forest. On hearing the news, Hitler expressed his joy and deep satisfaction in a speech at the Hofbräuhaus.

Nor did Hitler shirk from getting directly involved in the dirty work of Weimar politics. In August 1921 he led a squad of his followers into a beer cellar to disrupt a speech by the Bavarian League, a group that wanted to create a more autonomous Bavaria within a loose federal German state. The League's speaker, Otto Ballerstedt, was beaten up and Hitler ended the evening under questioning at police headquarters. On 14 September, Hitler himself physically attacked and badly injured Ballerstedt at the Löwenbräukeller. He was angry at the content of Ballerstedt's speech and, it was said, jealous of the fluency and power of his oratory. Hitler was arrested, found guilty of public nuisance and sentenced to 100 days in Stadelheim Prison. He was also ordered to pay a 1,000 mark fine. Much later, in June 1934, Hitler would get his revenge when he settled many old scores in the purge remembered as the Night of the Long Knives. Ballerstedt was murdered, probably at Dachau in Bavaria, and his body was dumped in nearby woods.

Hitler gained much useful knowledge from these early beer hall skirmishes. Above all, he learned from the two shots that just missed him on 4 November 1921. Hitler liked to think that he was protected by his sense of destiny, but after his close brush with death in the Hofbräuhaus he knew he also had to give serious thought to protecting himself from assassins.

Protecting the Führer

In his first few months as leader of the Nazi Party, Hitler's first line of protection was the loaded gun that he visibly carried on his hip. His second line of defence was the gang of old comrades, cronies and political allies he had gathered around him. This unofficial inner core of the NSDAP could be seen most days hanging around the reserved tables in their leader's favourite Munich haunts: Osteria Bavaria where Hitler usually had lunch when he was in the city, Café Heck off Ludwigstrasse where he enjoyed tea in the afternoons and Café Neumayr near the city food market and the Hofbräuhaus. In these relatively safe havens he was guarded by watchful, committed Hitlerites, all of whom were armed. In addition to Maurice and Hess, these cronies included Hitler's former sergeant in the army, Max Amann, the one-eyed anti-communist brawler Christian Weber, who liked to carry a rhino whip or riding crop whenever he was patrolling the streets of Munich and the popular wrestler Ulrich Graf, who made sure that a couple of muscle-men with army experience were always on call when Hitler needed them. In the official Nazi version of the Party's history, another layer of protection for Hitler began to coalesce around Emil Maurice in late 1920.

Stormtroopers!

This was the *Sturmabteilung* (SA) or Storm Detachment, initially known with a rare flash of Nazi humour as the NSDAP Gymnastics and Sports Division. In the early days it was sometimes simply called the Hitler Guard to differentiate it from other SA groups that had nothing to do with Hitler. The Nazis had no copyright on a term that had originated in the Kaiser's army in the 1914–18 war. The first Storm Detachments had been small squads of elite, specialized German shock troops trained to punch holes deep into the Allied line and break through the heavily protected trenches. After the war, the name was used by the Bavarian Social Democrats for their group of around 4,000 men who acted as protective guards and stewards at socialist rallies and meetings in the chaotic post-war years.

The development of the National Socialist SA owed much to Hermann Ehrhardt, a wealthy supporter of right-wing causes who had links to the emerging fascists in Italy. He had established the terrorist Organization Consul, which was probably behind the killing of Erzberger and was definitely responsible for the death of Walther Rathenau, the German–Jewish Foreign Minister of the young Weimar Republic in 1922. Ehrhardt provided Hitler with money and also expertise in the form of Hans Ulrich Klintzsch, a young enthusiastic marine

Hitler is shown in 1925 wearing traditional Bavarian costume favoured by German hill country people and popular with the beer-drinking fraternity. He is pictured with, left to right, Emil Maurice, Herman Kriebel, Rudolf Hess and Friedrich Weber.

officer who set about organizing a right-wing SA for protective and disruptive duties on the streets and in the beer halls of Munich. It would be at the disposal of both Ehrhardt and Hitler.

At first, this right-wing *Sturmabteilung* was poorly equipped. Most of its members were only armed with truncheons and small knives, they lacked a proper uniform and they turned up for duty in their civilian clothes garnished with a swastika armband. The bulk of them were barely out of their teens and Commander Klintzsch was only 22 himself. Nevertheless, Hitler saw the tremendous potential of the organization and in the following year, as soon as funds allowed, 240 young SA 'troops' were supplied with their first uniforms. It was based on the fashionable skiwear of the period: grey ski-cap, windbreaker jacket and tough riding pants. They were also given bicycles to improve their mobility around the streets of Munich. Hitler took care to attend their meetings regularly and seized every opportunity to inspire these young men to commit 'acts of national defence' against any Jews and socialists they encountered. On 4 November 1921, in the victorious Battle of the Hofbräuhaus, the SA confirmed its usefulness and its loyalty to Hitler. This new Hitler Guard would be a key tool for spreading the ideas of the fledgling Nazi Party and protecting its leader, at least until he had the time and resources to build a more effective security machine.

In the ancient language of Sanskrit the swastika means 'wellbeing', but the Nazis made it a symbol of evil.

CHAPTER 2

1923–33

Random Shots

In late April in the chaotic year of 1923, a smart red Mercedes containing two men was hurtling northwards towards Berlin. The car was travelling rather too fast for the poor road conditions. Near Leipzig, the driver spotted a roadblock up ahead. As he slowed, he realized that the men standing around the barrier were armed. They were also wearing red armbands to demonstrate their allegiance to the KPD, the German Communist Party. The driver was Ernst Hanfstaengl, a 36-year-old businessman of German origin who had spent much of his life in the USA and spoke both German and American English as a result. He showed the men his US passport and explained that he was an American paper manufacturer looking to invest in Germany. To curry favour with the armed men standing around his car, he added that he was hoping to create well-paid jobs for unemployed young men. The character in the passenger seat, a tired, pallid fellow with a short moustache who was wrapped up in a drab overcoat, was one of his employees. Convinced that the two men in the car were harmless, the armed men waved them on their way. If they had recognized the exhausted Hitler, they would have shot him on the spot.

Shots from all directions

It was not the only brush with death that Hitler would have in that frenetic year. At least three assassins would try to kill him in 1923: one in Thuringia, one in Leipzig and one in Tübingen. On two of these occasions shots were fired at him while he was travelling in his car. The third attempt on his life came while he was addressing a crowd. After each attack, close friends and followers urged him to take more care over his security in public places, but Hitler liked to laugh off their concerns. In private, however, he took their advice on board and new Nazi organizations would be created for his protection. Hitler was keen to project an image of himself as an unstoppable force, a heroic victor who had survived four years of trench warfare as well as countless street battles against his communist foes. But he also wanted to be seen as a leader who was popular. As much as was feasible, he had to be seen at ease among his own people. Too many guards surrounding him would dilute his political appeal as a dynamic man of action and he knew from his reading of history that no amount of security guards could ever stop a determined assassin getting through to his target. Instead he trusted in his deep sense of destiny for protection while developing his own private strategies for avoiding the killer's bullet. They would prove to be very effective over the next 20 years.

The price of success

By summer 1932 Hitler was close to fulfilling his dream. His party was working with an ever-increasing sense of purpose towards the Reichstag elections which would take place on the last day of July. Hitler and his followers knew they had a strong chance of becoming the largest party in Germany and taking some share of the government. Anyone with an interest in German politics could sense that the swastika was about to cast its jagged shadow over the land. Naturally, his impending triumph horrified his opponents and spurred many to direct action. That summer saw a return to the levels of political terror that Germany had suffered in the first years after the lost war. In July alone there were 86 deaths from acts of political violence. Of these, 30 were KPD members and 38 were Nazi supporters. The Nazi hierarchy itself admitted to being aware of more than 15 plots against their leader in the period from summer 1932 to the summer of 1934. On most of these occasions, shots were fired at Hitler as his car sped by en route to his next engagement. There were almost certainly many other planned attacks that the Nazi leadership knew nothing about.

He was no safer if he travelled by train. On 15 March 1932, Hitler needed to travel from Munich to Weimar, where he planned to speak about his relative success in the preliminary presidential election two days earlier. With over 11 million votes, he had come in a good second so had qualified to run in the second ballot against the venerable incumbent, Field Marshal Hindenburg. On this occasion Hitler had decided to make the 250-mile (400-km) journey by train rather than by car: he needed to discuss the fine tuning of this crucial speech with his travelling companions, Joseph Goebbels and Wilhelm Frick, then Minister of the Interior in Thuringia. They were both dynamic and skilful speakers and Hitler valued their advice. Their discussion was suddenly interrupted, however, by several shots, which shattered a window in their carriage. This was no random assault. The gunmen had known exactly which carriage contained the three Nazis and had planned accordingly. Only the speed of the train along that stretch of the line had resulted in the bullets missing the actual area where the three men were sitting.

A rowdy crowd

Hitler probably came closest to meeting a public death in the run-up to election day in 1932. On 29 July he visited the city of Freiburg on the western edge of the Black Forest. Close to France and Switzerland and long a magnet for wealthy international tourists from all over Europe, and especially Britain, cosmopolitan Freiburg was not natural electoral territory for the Nazis. It was, therefore, exactly the kind of place that Hitler wanted to win over to his cause. But on that day his powers of persuasion failed to cast their usual spell and the crowd was quiet and seemed bored. In his defence, it was his third major speech of the day and his 45th since the election campaign had begun two weeks earlier. The crowd listened dutifully but without the expected levels of intensity and enthusiasm.

Suddenly a shower of rocks emerged from the assembled gathering and flew towards the astonished orator and his attendants standing by his car, one missile striking him on the head and stunning him badly. The local police and SS guards established a cordon and restored calm while Hitler licked his wounds and quickly departed for the pretty spa town of Radolfzell on Lake Constance, where he hoped for a warmer welcome and a comfortable night's rest. When Nazi propagandists later described the fracas in Freiburg they would, of course, depict Hitler leaping from his car and advancing steadfastly towards the vile communists and Jews who had dared to disrupt his day, armed only with his rhino whip.

Ambushed by his own men

Hitler was in fact lucky to be contesting the election at all. He had already evaded a dangerous attack on 20 July in Pomerania, on the northern coast of Germany. Travelling by car near the old Hansa town of Stralsund, his driver had begun to brake before entering a tight hairpin bend when a volley of shots burst across the road. This was a carefully planned ambush, with several gunmen waiting at that critical point in Hitler's journey. They knew he would be coming in that direction and had chosen their spot well. Although many citizens in the relatively poor region of Pomerania supported the KPD, Hitler reckoned that this attack on his life had not been organized by his communist enemies. He was convinced it was an inside job. Many of the rank and file in his own brown-shirted SA were becoming discontented with their Great Leader.

In the Depression years in the early 1930s, many of Hitler's original followers were increasingly attracted to radical voices within the Nazi Party, such as Ernst Röhm and the Strasser brothers. They emphasized the socialistic elements that had been part of the original NSDAP message. These 'left-wing' Nazis were calling for a National Socialist revolution that would redistribute land and other assets in their direction. For over a decade, the SA had loyally provided the muscle to clear Hitler's path to power, but many of its members sensed a change in Hitler's political direction as he edged closer to the Reich Chancellery. He seemed to be in danger of becoming a puppet of the traditional establishment of wealthy industrialists and old generals.

As he sped away from the hairpin ambush towards his next speaking engagement near Rostock, Hitler could not really have known who the gunmen were that day, but it suited his longer-term plans to blame dissidents within the SA. When the German public went to the polls the following day, Hitler was by then in Nuremberg. He was thanking Party workers for their efforts when yet another bullet came in his direction but again missed its target. Once he was in power after 30 January 1933, he would feel safer from random shots such as these. As Chancellor, he enjoyed not just the protection offered by his own Nazi organizations but also the added security of the state police protection apparatus. Yet even then, not long after he assumed the chancellorship, nothing prevented a gunman in the NSDAP stronghold of Rosenheim from shooting at his car as he collected friends in a quiet residential street en route to his summer house in Obersalzberg.

A chariot fit for a Führer

Between 1925 and 1933, Hitler travelled ceaselessly around Germany on an almost perpetual election campaign. His pioneering use of aircraft enabled him suddenly to appear anywhere in Germany. It famously won him the admiration of many German voters and set him apart from most other staid leaders of the

Members of the SA, the paramilitary wing of the Nazi Party, at a gathering in the early 1930s. The strong-arm tactics of the SA stormtroopers had proved crucial to Hitler's rise to power.

time. Most of his travelling, however, was done by car. The Nazi Party claimed that he travelled more than 1.5 million km (932,000 miles) by car between the relaunch of the NSDAP in 1925 and becoming Chancellor in 1933. This was probably an exaggeration, but he certainly spent long days and nights motoring across the country on roads that had yet to be modernized by his government. His choice of car after 1930 also helps to explain why so many random shooting incidents came to nothing. Mercedes-Benz would deliver 44 specially modified vehicles for use by the Führer and his most senior colleagues between 1933 and 1945.

In the 1930s his vehicles of choice were the Mercedes 770K and, later, the sleeker 540K24. All of these had thickened, bullet-proof windscreens, steel armour and multi-chambered bullet-proof tyres. Eight-cylinder engines allowed for speeds of over 95 mph (153 kph) and later supercharged models could transport their four tons of weight at 110 mph (177 kph) for short distances at least: enough to escape from an ambush. Many of his cars were also fitted with steel armour under the chassis, to guard against exploding mines, and most had a convenient arsenal compartment containing spare weapons and ammunition. The thickness of steel used to protect the mobile Führer probably indicates the dwindling inner confidence of the Nazi regime over the period of the Third Reich. In Hitler's first years in power, 4 mm (0.16 in) steel was used to protect him but this later increased to 8 mm (0.32 in) when the war began in 1939; after Stalingrad, it rose to 18 mm (0.71 in) . Nevertheless, even the thinner armour used in his first Mercs was enough to protect him from bullets fired from a pistol or a rifle and it would save him from all but the closest bomb blast. Ironically, much of the protective technology developed by Mercedes-Benz took its lead from experimental work first undertaken for the notorious American gangster Al Capone during the Prohibition Era.

Comrades at the wheel

Hitler could trust his cars not to let him down and he could also rely on the five men whom he personally selected to act as his drivers between 1925 and 1945. His first two chauffeurs, Emil Maurice and Julius Schreck, had been with him from the very beginning. Maurice had joined the proto-Nazi DAP only a few weeks after Hitler in late 1919 and Schreck was member number 53 of the new NSDAP in 1920. Both men played a major role in developing the institutions of the Nazi movement. Schreck was a founding member of the SA and Maurice was its first leader. Both were early members of the SS, as was Anton Loibl who served as Hitler's reserve chauffeur throughout much of the 1920s. All three of these men took part in the 1923 Beer Hall Putsch and did time alongside Hitler in Landsberg Prison.

Although the fourth chauffeur, Sepp Dietrich, joined the Nazi Party relatively late in 1928, he quickly gained Hitler's trust and friendship. Like Hitler he had served throughout all four years of the First World War and had won the Iron Cross twice. An intelligent, ruthless man who rapidly advanced through the ranks of the SS, in due course he commanded Hitler's personal bodyguard, the elite Leibstandarte SS Adolf Hitler. In this role he had almost unparalleled access to the Führer on a daily basis. Dietrich repaid Hitler's trust in him in late June 1934, when he played a major role in the bloody elimination of the 'errant' SA leadership.

The fifth chauffeur, Erich Kempka, was a much younger SS officer with good practical skills in administration and a thorough training as a car mechanic. At first he acted as a reserve chauffeur, charged with making sure that the eight main vehicles in Hitler's fleet were deployed across Germany to mesh with the leader's demanding travel schedule. But when Schreck died suddenly in 1936, Kempka took a permanent place behind the Führer's wheel. Hitler enjoyed his company and over time Kempka became a useful member of Hitler's court. His last duty was to assist in the cremation of Hitler and Eva Braun in the Reich Chancellery garden on the final day of April 1945.

The car fanatic

In addition to absolute loyalty to Hitler and the Nazi cause, these five men were skilled, fast drivers and they all spent time familiarizing themselves with the vehicles in the Hitler fleet. The mechanic Kempka, in particular, was known to take a deep interest in the design of Hitler's 'wagons' and liked to discuss innovations and modifications with the engineers at Mercedes-Benz. It was said that he personally tested the steel used for bullet-proofing them with his own Luger. All five were also men who could handle themselves well in a tight situation such as an ambush or, as happened at least twice, in a bad accident. Hitler got away with a shoulder injury on 13 March 1930 when his car collided at speed with a heavy truck and in winter 1931 his car skidded into a tree, again at speed. He emerged from this accident with little more than a broken finger.

His love of fast cars played a large part in both accidents, as he would chide his drivers if they drove too slowly. He was an avid fan of motor-racing and took great pleasure in opening the 1936 International Automobile Exhibition in Berlin. But he was appalled at the loss of life on German roads throughout the 1930s and he eventually brought in draconian speed regulations to reduce the number of accidents, which he saw as causing an unpardonable loss of good Aryan blood. The maximum speed on his burgeoning autobahn network was a mere 56 mph (90 kph), reduced in the war to 50 mph (80 kph) to conserve fuel. However, his own drivers were ordered to ignore the restrictions and keep their foot down on the open road.

The five chauffeur/bodyguards had their work cut out when driving Hitler in urban locations. Here the Führer often preferred to travel in one of his beautiful midnight blue cabriolets. These were used for urban parades, where Hitler enjoyed standing and taking the salute of the crowd. Even when seated he insisted that the roof stay down, making himself an easy target for any marksman operating from above street level, or for a casually tossed grenade. On these occasions he trusted in his belief in his destiny, but he encouraged all of his senior staff to travel in a 'panzerized' Mercedes for safety. He ordered additional customized cars from the company as gifts for his most important allies; Mussolini, General Franco and the Portuguese dictator Salazar. One unused Mercedes kept under wraps was said to have been set aside for ultimate despatch to London. Once Britain was brought into the German sphere of influence, the Duke of Windsor would need it when he was restored to his rightful position as King Edward VIII.

CHAPTER 3

January 1932

The Kaiserhof Incident

In September 1930 the National Socialist Party was unexpectedly looking for new headquarters – in Berlin. Since its beginnings as the *Deutsche Arbeiterpartei* or German Workers' Party in 1919, it had been based in Munich, using a succession of ever-larger side-rooms and offices as its membership and finances grew. In 1931 it moved into its famous Brown House, a spacious three-storey mansion near the centre of the city, thanks to donations from generous supporters. The house was actually bought in 1930, but its opening was delayed because of the meticulous attention that the keen amateur architect Adolf Hitler lavished on its renovation. In the meantime, events had convinced Hitler that he now had to transport himself and his Party organization from its roots in Bavaria to the national capital, 360 miles (580 km) to the north in Prussia. The Party needed to find a large base in Berlin, for it had just made stunning gains in the Reichstag election held on 14 September.

Two years earlier, in the spring election of 1928, the NSDAP had seemed to be fading away. The German economy continued to strengthen, bolstered by American loans and the general optimism of 'the Roaring Twenties'; the dangerous firebrand Hitler and his stormtroopers were tarred with the chaos and violence of a bitter post-war moment that was now passing into history. Despite a vigorous campaign, in 1928 they only gathered a miserable 2.6 per cent of the votes cast. But in 1930 the global depression saw the Nazis rise suddenly to become the second-largest political party in Germany. Their number of seats in the national parliament soared from 12 to 107 and their share of the popular vote grew almost eightfold to well over six million.

Hitler had been transformed from a regional curiosity into a figure of national significance and now he needed to be in Berlin, right at the heart of the wheeling and dealing, the plotting and manoeuvring of Weimar politics. Nazi leaders in Munich and Berlin both agreed on the ideal location for their new HQ. It had to be in the largest, the best-equipped, the most modern and the most luxurious accommodation in Germany, if not Europe: the Hotel Excelsior.

The price of dissent

The transformation of the Hotel Excelsior from a failing business into one of the top hotels in the world was effected by a virtuoso hotelier named Curt Elschner, who was inspired by the new deluxe hotels being built in the USA. The Excelsior offered 600 rooms, nine restaurants and a very long list of amenities and services for its guests. Its library stocked hundreds of daily newspapers and weekly magazines from around the globe. All of its systems were powered by electricity, including the various technologies available at the state-of-the-art spa facility built into its basement. And above all it was linked by an impressive underpass to the nearby Anhalter Bahnhof railway terminus, south of Potsdamer Platz. Guests at the Excelsior could buy their tickets in the hotel and proceed to their train compartment without coming into contact with the unpredictable street life above. This last feature especially appealed to Hitler's guards, who were concerned for the security of their Führer and other Nazi top brass in a city that, unlike Munich, had a reputation as a fervent stronghold of the Left.

The Excelsior was not the most prestigious hotel in Berlin – that was the Adlon by the Brandenburg Gate – but it was the best option in the eyes of the Nazi hierarchy. There was only one problem: Elschner refused to rent a floor of his hotel to them. He would suffer for his decision to turn down the Nazi request. All Nazi Party officials and members were instantly forbidden to enter the Excelsior and, once Hitler was in power, the hotel was raided. Numerous 'offensive' artworks were removed from its grand hall, which bore the unfortunate name of the Hall of Free Thought and contained images of historical thinkers, some of Jewish origin. These were replaced with portraits of National Socialist intellectuals. In due course, Elschner fled Germany to avoid being liquidated.

Hotel Kaiserhof

The Nazis were made much more welcome at the Kaiserhof on Wilhelmstrasse. Its owners publicly demonstrated their hostility to the Weimar government by flying the old black, white and red flag of the German Empire above the hotel entrance rather than the black, red and gold of the Weimar Republic. The foyer also boasted photographs of Kaiser Wilhelm I visiting the newly opened hotel in 1871. Very soon an entire upper floor of the Kaiserhof had been transformed into a busy Nazi command post with telephones, typewriters and all the paraphernalia of a political party headquarters – complete with boxes of truncheons and pistol ammunition. Now the foyer was crammed every day with SS and SA uniformed guards and lingering journalists hoping to snatch a word with Hitler's press agent, Otto Dietrich, or Ernst Hanfstaengl, now head of the Nazi Foreign Press Bureau. As Hitler became increasingly embroiled in the negotiations for high office under President Hindenburg, he spent more time working at the Kaiserhof. He lived there continually from August 1932 until his eventual appointment as Chancellor six months later.

This was where he directed the two Reichstag election campaigns that year, following which the NSDAP emerged as the largest party in Germany. It was also in the Kaiserhof that he faced down the almost fatal threat to his leadership from the dynamic Gregor Strasser, restoring full control over the Nazi movement with one of the most passionate speeches of his entire political career. Here he also attended the regular meetings held in the Kaiserhof by the National Club, an exclusive organization consisting of wealthy German industrialists who met informally with senior Nazi officials involved with industrial and economic matters. Many leading Nazis took permanent rooms in the hotel to be close to Hitler, often meeting to talk politics and plan tactics in the adjacent Viennese café.

At a short ceremony in the Kaiserhof, Hitler finally became a German citizen in February 1932. For almost seven years he had been a stateless immigrant, having renounced his Austrian citizenship in 1925, shortly after his release from Landsberg Prison. His convenient 'appointment' to a spurious post in the staunchly Nazi city of Braunschweig allowed him to complete the necessary forms so that he could run in the forthcoming presidential election. In many ways, the period in the Kaiserhof was crucial for the Party and for its Führer, not least because he could look out from it every day to the target of his ambition, the Reich Chancellery directly opposite the hotel.

A poisoned dish?

As in Munich, Hitler liked to eat surrounded by his court, a mixture of old cronies and personal bodyguards, members of his personal staff and those who were involved in projects of current interest to him. Both lunch and dinner were taken quite late in the day to fit in with the Führer's distinct body-clock. Although no gourmand, Hitler enjoyed long sessions at the meal table, which gave him a chance to quiz new faces in his group and, more often, expound at length on his personal thoughts and ideas. After one lunch in January 1932, which had stretched well beyond an hour, the faces around the table began to turn pallid. The entire group dining with Hitler that day fell ill almost simultaneously, struck by waves of extreme nausea and unsteadiness. Most were soon experiencing acute stomach cramps and vomiting prolifically and one in particular was seriously unwell. This was Hitler's chief adjutant, Wilhelm Brückner, an *Alte Kämpfer* or old warrior from the 1923 Munich Putsch and one of six old comrades who served as Hitler's ceremonial honour guard by virtue of their length of service to the Party. He was a fit man, but after his meal that day he spent several weeks in hospital recovering from a violent attack of food poisoning. Although none died, all of the other guests at Hitler's table that afternoon were ill for several days. The least affected figure at the table was Hitler himself, possibly because he chose to eat sparingly during the day and usually restricted himself to a light vegetarian dish when lunching in public.

As a keen student of history, from his earliest days in politics Hitler had always been careful about what he ate. He well understood why colourless and odourless white arsenic was called 'the king of poisons and the poison of kings'. His friend and confidant Ernst Hanfstaengl recalled the many birthday cakes and chocolates that arrived at Hitler's flat in Munich on 20 April 1923, apparently sent by some of his many female admirers. Hitler refused to touch them and after a note had been made of the senders' details, all were thrown out.

Taking better care of the Führer

Was the Kaiserhof incident a deliberate attack against Hitler or simply the result of 'normal' food contamination? Little documentation concerning the incident survives although after the war one contemporary remembered that a trace of poison had been found in the remains of the meal and in samples taken from the affected diners. A full investigation of the kitchen staff was undertaken but no one was arrested. Magda Goebbels was in no doubt, however, that an attempt had been made to kill her beloved Führer. For the next year, until Hitler entered the Reich Chancellery, his most devoted female admirer made it her personal duty to feed Hitler whenever he was in Berlin. She supervised all the snacks and meals prepared for him in the Kaiserhof kitchens.

The new German Chancellor, Adolf Hitler, greets President von Hindenburg in Berlin in 1933. Bringing up the rear are Hermann Göring and Joseph Goebbels (in top hat).

For Hitler, avoiding the poison attack which had laid his subordinates low was yet another sign that his victorious destiny was preordained. But he also learned to keep his most trusted cooks close to him. When he became Chancellor, he brought his old cook from the Brown House in Munich to supervise his private kitchen in Berlin. The trusted Anni Döhring remained senior cook at the Berghof until the very end of the Reich. He especially valued his final chef in the Berlin Führerbunker, Constanze Manziarly, and sat with her eating his last ever meal on the day he blew his brains out.

Hitler's minders shuddered at the ease with which their leader had been exposed to danger in the Kaiserhof and they set about planning additional layers of security. Over time they would throw an ever-widening safety net around every aspect of his daily life. By 1942, when he spent most of his time at his Eastern Front command posts, such as Wolf's Lair in East Prussia, the SS was using food-tasters to check all of Hitler's meals. These were seldom enthusiastic 'volunteers' but usually press-ganged Polish or Russian prisoners, or just naive youngsters, as the survivor Margaret Wölk later testified. She and some friends in her East Prussian village were young Germans who just happened to be available when the SS came looking for tasters. Although they were grateful for food that far exceeded the wartime norms, they were terrified at the thought of sudden death by a poison that might have been introduced into Hitler's diet by the Allies, by partisans or even by dissident Germans.

But on the night of 30 January 1933, in earlier, happier times for the Nazi cause, Hitler returned in triumph to the Hotel Kaiserhof. He had just been appointed to the post of Chancellor by Hindenburg. As he stepped out of the lift on the floor that housed the Nazi HQ, he was met by a guard of honour drawn from the hotel's staff: managers, cooks, maids and waiters, all greeting the man of the hour. A shrewd SS officer in the official bodyguard might have scanned that line of excited faces and wondered if it contained the Kaiserhof poisoner.

CHAPTER 4

1933
The Fake Stormtrooper

itler loved the high meadowlands of beautiful Obersalzberg. He first visited the area in 1923 to spend time with his friend and mentor Dietrich Eckart, and soon fell in love with its peerless scenery, fresh air and the sense of space between the lakelands near Munich to the north and the snow-tipped Alps to the south. After his release from Landsberg Prison in December 1924, he rented a small cabin in the valley to finish the second part of his political testament, *Mein Kampf*. Then from 1928 onwards he rented a summer house called Haus Wachenfeld, inviting his half-sister Angela and her daughter Geli to run the small household for him. The initial sales of his book were disappointing and they remained so until his star began to rise after the 'breakthrough' election in September 1930. But Hitler had many important admirers with deep pockets who appreciated that this political firebrand needed a place to step back from the pressures of political life and recharge his batteries. At Obersalzberg he could read, think, listen to music and relax.

By 1933 the new Chancellor, soon dictator, of Germany had amassed more than enough royalties to purchase the house outright. A sudden rush to buy *Mein Kampf* when its author came to power had made him very wealthy. He now began to buy out his neighbours and started to consider remodelling his rather modest residence into an imposing mountain retreat worthy of a Great Leader. By 1936 Haus Wachenfeld would be transformed into the fabled Berghof or Mountain Court, which impressed visiting world leaders as much as the audiences who caught a brief glimpse of its luxury on cinema newsreels.

Hitler particularly liked to be filmed gazing out from its vast retractable window to the mountains beyond, or relaxing with guests on the imposing terrace. The Berghof compound had its own airstrip, which after 1939 was heavily defended with anti-aircraft guns and machines that manufactured smoke as camouflage. Like many of the Hollywood stars he so admired, Hitler's 'villa' was equipped with its own movie theatre. But in 1933 the Berghof was still a relatively small chalet residence, little different from the other summer houses dotted around the valley. And it certainly had less privacy than the homes of the cinema celebrities in Beverly Hills.

Guten Morgen, Herr Hitler

It may well have been Hitler's preferred holiday spot, but living at Haus Wachenfeld exposed him to considerable risk, especially between 1928 and 1935 when the security arrangements there were rudimentary. His own landholding around the house was initially quite small and although it was fenced off there were other properties within view. It took a little time for all of his neighbours to accept that his offer to buy them out could not be refused. The hillside around the house was also criss-crossed by a network of public trails, which were popular with picnickers and hillwalkers for much of the year. And a wide, much-used pathway passed directly in front of the house, within a hundred yards or so of the door.

Hitler used these tracks on a daily basis when he emerged with friends to walk, chat and expound his ideas during an hour or so of fresh air and exercise. Many local and foreign ramblers, including a number of startled British holidaymakers, found themselves bumping into the Nazi leader and his entourage in the late 1920s and well into the 1930s. Many later recounted how pleasant and courteous the great man was towards his fellow walkers and how much interest he had taken in their holiday plans in Germany. Photographs from before 1936 show the friendly crowds that regularly gathered throughout the summer at the fence by Hitler's gate. It was not unusual for Hitler to walk down to the path with only a couple of SS men at his side and engage in some light banter with his 'fans'. He rebuffed all advice to surround himself with a larger contingent of security men on these occasions. Here, deep in this Austro-Germanic heartland, he wanted to be seen as a statesman at ease among his people. Excellent public relations perhaps, but a nightmare for his bodyguards.

Hitler looks across to the Obersalzberg Mountains from the balcony of the Berghof, his country retreat near Berchtesgaden.

Sniper country

Hitler's decision to locate his summer headquarters on the Obersalzberg was based upon his love of the romantic Alpine world and its association with the many German composers, artists, poets and thinkers who had been inspired there. It made little sense in terms of security. The hilly landscape, rugged and irregular at higher altitudes, was heavily forested, so it was a very difficult environment for guards to cover and monitor. It provided myriad possibilities for an intruder trained in making the best use of the lie of the land. The Berghof estate eventually measured almost 8 km^2 (3 miles^2), requiring regular patrols around its lengthy fenced perimeter. Up until 1935, any patient and determined trespasser had a chance of making his way through the defences to find a viable position for a shot at Hitler wandering about in his domain. By late 1936, however, Martin Bormann, the Nazi overseer at the Berghof, had used the threat of armed intruders to convince Hitler to let him transform this holiday home into a fortress with its own resident garrison of men from the elite regiment Leibstandarte SS Adolf Hitler.

Despite this improved protection, the Führer continued to offer reasonable opportunities to a sniper by refusing to use the secure and defensible mountain-top Kehlsteinhaus or Eagle's Nest that Bormann had specially constructed for him. He much preferred to amble along to his favourite bolt-hole, the Mooslahnerkopf Teehaus. The path up to the cold and misty Eagle's Nest was steep and exposed to the elements, but the 3 km (2 mile) walk to and from the Teehaus, although longer, was through gentler, lightly wooded, lower terrain that Hitler found much more pleasing.

A Brownshirt with a gun

The very real dangers Hitler faced while living at Obersalzberg were fully exposed in 1933, when his guards began to notice a man in the uniform of an SA stormtrooper. He was observed repeatedly walking around the Berghof perimeter, taking a suspicious interest in its fences and gates. Once detained and searched, he was found to be carrying a loaded pistol and couldn't confirm details of his SA membership. Assumed to be an assassin, he promptly disappeared to a destination and a fate unknown. Hitler was so worried by the sudden appearance of this fake stormtrooper that he had a unit of his best SS men sent to Obersalzberg immediately. In 1939, Bridget Dowling, Hitler's Irish sister-in-law, published a book about her connection to the Führer in which she said she had been living at the Berghof in the mid-1930s. She claimed to have witnessed an incident there in which an SA stormtrooper called Kraus fired a shot at Hitler before being gunned down by five SS guards. However, Bridget's colourful tales of her time in Nazi Germany were written in 1939 when she was living in America. She was short of money and desperate to cash in on her relative's notoriety, so it's likely that the Kraus story was the product of a ghostwriter's imagination.

There were, however, genuine would-be assassins who recognized Hitler's vulnerability on the Obersalzberg. In 1938, the hapless Swiss student Maurice Bavaud spent several days in the vicinity of the Berghof looking for an opportunity to assassinate Hitler. During the war, at least one dissident German army officer suspected that Hitler could be caught off guard in the relaxed atmosphere of his mountain complex, and planned accordingly. And though the British Special Operations Executive (SOE) considered several assassination scenarios in different parts of the Reich, its planners concluded that the Berghof offered the best chance for a successful kill. Doubtless they had all read Geoffrey Household's 1939 thriller novel, *Rogue Male*, which begins with a British sportsman 'holidaying' in the mountains of central Europe with an unnamed dictator in his sights.

CHAPTER 5

Spring 1933

Red Reaction

In 1933, Adolf Hitler would be murdered by a smiling blond maiden holding a bunch of flowers out towards him, but spraying him in the face with a secret phial of lethal prussic acid. A gift for the Führer, a highly expensive pen, was on its way in the mail from 'a devoted supporter'. It was primed to explode when the nib was pushed down firmly on to paper. A charming puppy gifted to Hitler by a wealthy admirer had unusually sharp claws: it had been injected with rabies. Staff on the Munich–Berlin railway had been bribed by British spies to drop water-soluble white arsenic into the tea and coffee urns in Hitler's train compartment. A self-destruct device had been built into Hitler's new personal aeroplane, the Junkers Ju 52 named *Immelmann II* after Germany's first Great War fighter ace. The device would activate automatically during Hitler's forthcoming 'Flight over Germany' election campaign. Soviet agents were planning to kidnap Hitler at his Alpine summer house and replace him with a specially groomed actor, an exiled German communist who happened to be a double for the Führer.

In the first months of 1933, a stream of letters and messages similar to these arrived on the desks of senior police officials throughout Germany. Most of the senders threatened, or simply warned against a more conventional assassination by grenade or sniper and they came from a bewildering range of countries around the world. They were evidence that Hitler had become a global celebrity of sorts and could expect the same sort of junk mail that entertainers and sportsmen were having to cope with. It was a time when the mass media were coming to the fore in public life. As a deeply divisive and controversial politician, Hitler could expect more than his fair share of letters from cranks and bitter antagonists in his postbag, even though most of his mail in the early days of the Third Reich seems to have come from admirers, especially women. Police officials buckled down to the task of sifting through mountains of mail in search of the truly dangerous correspondent, but inevitably they found that only a very small number of the messages received merited any further investigation. Most were from fantasists or the disgruntled who were just letting off steam. Naturally, none of these communications came from sources that were most likely to be actually plotting against Hitler and his new regime.

Crushing the communists

As Hitler gradually assumed ever greater powers in the early months of 1933, many observers expected the strongest resistance to the Nazi takeover to come from its most bitter ideological foe – the German Communist Party or KPD. It was the strongest communist party in western Europe and was well organized and well led. In the election on 6 November 1932, the KPD won almost six million votes and gained 100 deputies in the Reichstag. Five months later, in the last 'free' election to be held in Weimar Germany, 81 KPD deputies were elected despite intense intimidation by the National Socialist street machine: in Prussia alone over 50,000 'assistant-police' helped to monitor the polling stations. They were easily identified by their white armbands, worn over their SA and SS uniforms. Those 81 elected KPD deputies never took their seats in Berlin. In many cases they were already on their way to prisons and camps throughout Germany.

Before the election campaign was over, an estimated 4,000 communists, lawyers, writers, journalists and academics had ended up in 'police custody', in most cases permanently. The KPD leader, Ernst Thälmann, was arrested two days before the poll and subjected to 11 years of solitary confinement which would only end with his summary execution at Buchenwald concentration camp in August 1944. Meticulously planned well in advance, the Nazi clampdown on the KPD was quick and efficient. Nevertheless, although its membership declined massively over the next 12 years of the Third Reich, the KPD never disappeared entirely. Some of its leaders escaped to exile in France or the Soviet Union, where they tried to maintain a viable underground network. But the structure that would have enabled the communists to maintain organized opposition to National Socialism within the Reich had been smashed in those first few weeks

Hitler's bodyguards had to be on high alert for potential attacks by assassins masquerading as admirers.

of 1933. Any future resistance to Hitler would have to come from individuals or tiny groups operating on their own initiative.

Death in the mail

Ten days after Hitler became Chancellor the police authorities in Berlin began to take an interest in a self-exiled émigré living in France. Ludwig Assner was quite well known to anyone who had taken an active role in the chaotic politics of post-war Bavaria back in November 1918. Assner first emerged in those momentous days after the Armistice, as Germany stumbled from Empire towards a new and uncertain republican future. The Kaiser abdicated and left for exile in the Netherlands and the 738-year rule of the Wittelsbach dynasty in Bavaria also came to a sudden end. The Bavarian king Ludwig III departed for Austria, and a group of socialists led by Kurt Eisner declared that Bavaria was now a free socialist republic.

At that point in his country's history, Ludwig Assner was a socialist and was sufficiently committed to that cause to serve as Eisner's chauffeur and bodyguard from November 1918 until Eisner's assassination three months later. By 1924, Assner had travelled right across the political spectrum. That year he stood in the Bavarian parliamentary elections as a candidate for the Völkisch-Social Block, a grouping of loosely allied conservative, nationalist and anti-Semitic parties. He was elected but was unable to take his seat on a technicality. He had been sentenced to four months in prison a few weeks before the election. From his cell in Landsberg Prison, even Hitler had protested that Assner's candidature was illegal. At some point Assner may have flirted with the idea of joining the NSDAP, but by 1933 he was living in France and his politics had changed direction yet again. He had taken a deep dislike to Hitler and the Nazis and had rediscovered some of his earlier left-wing fervour.

In February 1933, officials in the Bavarian section of the NSDAP were alerted by a telegram from an unknown source in France: Ludwig Assner was plotting to assassinate Germany's new Chancellor. Believing that Hitler would remember him, Assner had decided to send a letter to Berlin. It was private and it was poisoned. If it was ever sent, the technical basis for this proposed postal attack was never disclosed by the German authorities. The toxin ricin was well known by this period and the US Air Force had considered using it as a weapon in 1918. Nevertheless, it is difficult to imagine that an individual civilian such as Assner could have had access to such a restricted chemical. In any case, although opening and handling a letter soaked in a strong ricin solution was potentially very dangerous, unsolicited foreign mail would almost certainly have been screened by humble clerks long before reaching the Führer's fingers. Further investigation into Assner confirmed that he was definitely hostile towards Hitler. He feared that Hitler's belligerent policies would plunge Germany into a second European war. However, any serious concerns that the authorities had about Assner quickly evaporated when it was discovered that he was willing to abandon his assassination plans on receipt of a generous payment from Berlin. Assner was dismissed as not only a lone wolf but also possibly mad and certainly pathetic. The various German police organizations were more concerned by threats closer to home and from more credible, better organized would-be assassins.

The Königsberg cell

With Germany gripped in political crisis, President Hindenburg used his emergency powers to dissolve the Reichstag on the first day of February 1933. He called for fresh elections to be held in early March. Two weeks later, on 15 February, Hitler outlined his plans for his fifth *Deutschlandflug*, or aerial election campaign, which would allow him to speak directly to as many people as possible in the brief time available. He decided that his final speech of the campaign would take place in the old East Prussian capital city of Königsberg on 4 March, the eve of the poll. Hitler chose Königsberg as the venue for this key moment because its current predicament symbolized everything that Hitler hated about Weimar Germany. Königsberg was one of the most historic cities in Germany, having been the fortress base of the crusading Teutonic Knights who had established German domination over the western Slavs and much of the Baltic coastline in the Middle Ages. It had been a wealthy Hansa trading city and was a cultural centre with a famous university and a rich publishing heritage. Ever since Versailles, however, the city and the East Prussian lands around it had, in Hitler's words, 'been amputated from the body of the Reich' by the contentious strip of territory known as the Polish Corridor. By finishing his campaign in this politically charged spot, Hitler was reminding the German electorate of his pledge to bring all the German speakers scattered by the Treaty of Versailles back into one unified German state that was ethnically and geographically coherent.

Karl Lutter and his fellow conspirators noted that Hitler would be in their city in 17 days' time, in order to deliver a brief speech. He would only be there for several hours, before returning to Berlin for election day. Lutter was keen to provide a suitable conclusion to Hitler's election campaign, preferably one that would finish off Hitler himself. A seaman and shipwright in Königsberg, Lutter was a committed communist and the leader of a small party cell which hoped to position a bomb close to the platform where Hitler would deliver his speech. The group held two secret meetings in February to discuss the necessary details. They seem to have had the good sense to commit nothing of their plans to paper before they were arrested on the day before Hitler's arrival. However, the ease with which the underground Lutter Group was infiltrated by a police informer and then rounded up says much about the lack of operational experience in what remained of the KPD, at a point in time when its experienced leaders were being eliminated.

Fortunately for Lutter and his fellow conspirators, they were interrogated by the civil police rather than by the Nazi organizations, which had not quite taken over complete control in investigations of this kind. The police found little evidence to support a vigorous prosecution as the Lutter Group's two clandestine meetings had generated nothing to incriminate its members. There was no paper evidence and crucially there was no proof that they had acquired explosives. The arrested group members refused to confess and they maintained their innocence. At that point in the transition from a democratic republic to a totalitarian state, the police in Königsberg felt there was little more they could do but detain the men and wait for some evidence to turn up, but nothing did. In December, all members of the group were quietly released.

Ghosts of Germany past

The destruction of the Reichstag on 27 February 1933 by the Dutch communist Marinus van der Lubbe famously gave Hitler an opportunity to intensify the suppression of leftist opponents and extend his authority in defence of the Reich. As the Reichstag building was out of action, it also gave him an excuse to stage the opening of the newly elected parliament along National Socialist principles. Rather than the mundane filing-in and swearing-in of new deputies, Hitler planned a day of ceremony and ritual that would not just mark the birth of a New Germany but would also demonstrate a continuum with the best of the old. It would be held on 23 March: not in leftist Berlin but at Potsdam, the home of the great Prussian kings.

Hitler and the old, revered President Hindenburg would proceed in their motor cavalcade along Potsdam's broad avenues, swathed in alternating giant banners bearing the Nazi swastika and the Imperial flag, both in black, white

The destruction of the Reichstag gave Hitler the excuse to take the reins of power and be done with democratic hindrances.

and red. The two leaders would make their way to the Garrison Church, spiritual home of the German army and the site of the first Imperial Reichstag in 1871, held in the wake of Germany's crushing victory over France. Hitler and Hindenburg would process along the nave of the church towards the tombs of the 'Soldier King', Frederick William I, and his son, the magnificent Frederick the Great.

On the day, Hindenburg also stopped at the Imperial Gallery and nodded in silence towards the empty chair of the absent Kaiser-in-exile. Before the regal tombs, Hitler bowed deeply in an act of homage to the elderly president, who had been his commander in the Great War and was the living symbol of the vanished Second Reich that Hitler had volunteered to defend in 1914. Gently taking the frail old man's hand, Hitler led him down the marble steps to the sacred crypt below, where the two old soldiers stood and silently communed with the great ghosts of Germany's past. The Day of Potsdam was beautifully stage-managed by Goebbels. It signalled to the nation, and especially to the aristocratic officer class in the army, that Hitler was no revolutionary but a leader steeped in reverence for the Hohenzollern military tradition. Hitler was a man who could be trusted.

The tunnel bombers

Goebbels' stage directions did not go entirely to plan. They were tarnished by the unusually heavy-handed security arrangements that shrouded the town of Potsdam throughout the day. The police and the Nazi organizations on duty were unmistakably nervous, despite the political rituals taking place in a location that was relatively easy to monitor and supervise. Everyone was on special alert thanks to a disturbing discovery the previous day. A routine sweep through the cellars and foundations beneath the Garrison Church found evidence of recent digging, which led on to a freshly constructed tunnel that ran for several metres directly underneath the nave. The size of the tunnel suggested that several conspirators had been co-operating on the project. It was thought that the diggers intended to pack it with explosives and then detonate them during the coming ceremony. If so, the blast would have wiped out the country's top leaders and also many office-holders in the new government who were present at the great state occasion.

The discovery of the tunnel foiled one of the last chances to thwart the Nazi takeover of what remained of democratic Germany. Inevitably the NSDAP media machine blamed the communists, although there was little real proof that they had been involved, and no one, not even some token stooge, was ever arrested. But in the tense atmosphere of the time, it was enough to point the finger at the KPD. In any case, the tunnel was certainly a useful discovery, as it helped remind the population that only a strong Nazi government could protect them from the Red Terror.

On 23 March the Enabling Bill, which gave Hitler dictatorial powers, surged through the Reichstag by 441 votes to 94. The Social Democrats had been intimidated by the raucous, armed brown-shirted deputies in the chamber, led by Reichstag president Hermann Göring, and the remaining Centrists had been bought off by empty promises of future moderation from Hitler. There was no resistance from the KPD, for its 81 elected deputies were not present. The previous day, 22 March 1933, the leading communists in holding cells throughout the Reich had been transferred to a new special facility where they could be concentrated, detained and 're-educated' in one place. The camp lay outside a pretty medieval Bavarian town, then famous for its *fin de siècle* colony of avant-garde artists: Dachau.

From captain to comrade

After the almost instant transformation of Germany into a totalitarian dictatorship, plotters against Hitler of any kind had little chance of success. It didn't stop them trying, though, and KPD members and sympathizers tried harder than most. Like Ludwig Assner, Josef 'Beppo' Römer only found his true beliefs after a long political journey. Born in 1892, he belonged to the generation of young men who fought in the First World War and returned to a defeated Fatherland that was disintegrating. Römer had in fact enlisted in the army in 1911. With his pre-war experience in the ranks and his bourgeois background and education, he quickly became a popular and successful officer at the Front. Captain Römer was the kind of war-hardened professional soldier who carried on fighting long after his 'official' demobilization. Like most officers of his class, he sided with the paramilitary Freikorps against the Left and was one of the founding officers of the Bund Oberland Corps. The Bund helped crush the Bavarian Soviet Republic in spring 1919 and it played a vital role in the bitter fighting between German paramilitaries and Polish forces in 1921 over the rich territory of Upper Silesia. Römer's men distinguished themselves at the battle of Annaberg, as did a number of later prominent Nazis such as Hitler's chauffeur Sepp Dietrich and the commandant at Auschwitz, Rudolf Höss.

However, over time Römer's political thinking took a leftward direction. He sympathized with striking workers in 1921, refusing to shoot at them, and he opposed colleagues in the Bund who wanted closer co-operation with the rising NSDAP. By the late 1920s, Römer was acting as a lawyer, defending workers and helping them to join trades unions, and he was editor of the leftist magazine *Aufbruch* or New Departure. He may not have joined the KPD and any thoughts of plotting to kill Hitler that he had were probably academic, but as the leader of a small intellectual circle and a man with military expertise, Beppo Römer had become a figure of concern to the security agencies of the new Third Reich.

In 1934 Römer was arrested on suspicion of conspiracy and began a five-year tour of several Nazi prison camps, ending up in Dachau where he came into contact with many other oppositionists. His experience in the camps hardened his resolve to fight against the regime. At some point he crossed paths with Nikolaus von Halem, a judge of aristocratic origin who had refused to take the required oath of loyalty to the Führer. In 1939 Beppo was unexpectedly released. The authorities may have wanted to use him as bait to flush out bigger fish in the anti-Nazi underground. Römer was obviously aware that he was under surveillance but he persevered with his aim of setting up a small cell of activists. He made contact with Halem, who managed to supply some funding for a clandestine pamphlet called *Informationsdienst* or Information Service.

Römer also began talking about 'cutting off the snake's head' by assassinating Hitler. At this point, the undercover Gestapo agent in his group filed his report and Römer was arrested again for aiding and abetting the enemy. Once he was back in prison, the authorities could begin to probe for the names of those he had gathered around himself during his spell back 'outside'. In 1942 he was returned to Dachau. Like many other anti-Nazi activists, Beppo Römer continued to maintain some kind of personal resistance against Nazism and almost lived to see its downfall in May 1945. His struggle achieved little in concrete terms, but men and women like him were a persistent and worrying nuisance for the Nazi authorities and a constant reminder that their dread world-view was not shared by all Germans.

The British communist plot

During the 1930s, only one communist got close enough to Hitler to have a real chance of killing him. He was neither German nor Russian. (Allan) Alexander Foote was born in Lancashire, bred in Yorkshire and had a fair deal of Scottish blood running through his veins. Inevitably tough and gruff, Foote was one of the British volunteers who fought for the Spanish Republic against Franco. When the Spanish Civil War ended in April 1939, he carried on his own war against fascism by providing and passing on information to and from anti-Nazi resistance groups in Germany and Switzerland. Many pages have been written on the question of whether Foote was a formal Russian NKVD operative and/ or a British double agent. What is certain is that he realized that truly effective opposition to Hitler would only come from the Soviet Union, rather than from the spineless governments in Paris and London. During the war, he made a significant contribution to resistance communication networks within Germany, such as the Red Orchestra group of radio operators, and he certainly passed on information to Moscow via at least two Soviet espionage rings. In the late summer of 1939, he just happened to be in southern Germany, ostensibly on a cycling holiday around the Chiemsee and the other beautiful lakes south of Munich and taking the opportunity to improve his knowledge of German.

An extra two for lunch

After the war, Alex Foote claimed that he discovered the Osteria Bavaria on Munich's Schellingstrasse by accident, enticed to enter by its set tourist menu for the equivalent of one shilling and sixpence. If this was true, he must have been the only person in the city who didn't know that this Italian restaurant was the Führer's favourite haunt: he had been dining on their fine Alpine trout since 1920. He had wooed his only two serious girlfriends there – Marie 'Mitzi' Reiter and Eva Braun – and whenever he was in Bavaria it was his preferred spot for lunch or dinner. In the early 1920s, a younger Hitler had often partied at the Osteria Bavaria with his street gang of Nazi chums. By 1939, the 50-year-old Hitler tended to dine with smaller groups. Tucking in to his tourist menu fodder, Foote had numerous opportunities to watch the Führer come and go. He observed the Führer's well-known Austrian courtesy, bowing and kissing the hand of any lady guest and remaining standing until they were seated. Foote also noticed that he was sometimes only accompanied by two or three adjutants, although it had to be assumed that some of the restaurant's clients and its staff were there in a security capacity.

Countless foreign tourists in the 1930s caught a glimpse of the great man in the osteria, making his way to his strictly personal reserved table. Many of them were surprised at how relaxed Hitler seemed there and they also noticed that the security around him was remarkably casual. Foote also spotted that laxity and noted that there seemed to be no regular inspections of the restaurant by the SS. Foote mentioned his 'meetings' with Hitler to his Soviet contacts and Moscow sent him a companion, Len Buerton aka Len Brewer, a communist car mechanic from Reading who was also a radio operator with connections to Russian intelligence. The two British plotters were encouraged to consider the feasibility of an attack on Hitler while he was entangled in his pasta.

Foote and Buerton monitored Hitler's comings and goings, took details of the uniformed staff that attended him and made an estimate of the security staff that were 'in costume'. They mapped the layout of the osteria, recording its entrances and exits plus any obstacles or peculiarities that might impede an assassin intent on getting closer to the Führer. In the dossier that they sent to Moscow, they stressed their main findings. Naturally, Hitler liked to sit with his back to the wall so that he could scan the restaurant in front of him. The wall behind him was wood-panelled and painted with the usual bucolic mythological scenes of plenty and pleasure and behind the panelling was the thin interior plaster wall of a small and little-used cloakroom. If a bag or a case containing a time bomb was left there it would do a lot of damage to the adjacent dining room. There was a real chance of doing away with Hitler.

Foote and Buerton submitted their plans to Moscow and waited for the expected green light. And waited. But there was no response from the Kremlin. It was August 1939, when the 'Scum of the Earth' and the 'Bloody Assassin of the Workers' met and greeted each other in David Low's cartoon to discuss the dissection of Poland. On behalf of their masters, Ribbentrop and Molotov were just about to sign the treaty of non-aggression that ensured the disappearance of Poland from the map of Europe. Stalin had gone quite cold on the idea of spoiling Hitler's lunch.

CHAPTER 6

1930–34
Plots from Within

On the evening of 30 August 1930, two guards in the black uniform of the SS stood outside an arched doorway that straddled the corner junction of Hedemannstrasse and Wilhelmstrasse in central Berlin. The doorway was the pivotal entrance to a five-storey building that swept back in both directions along these two broad avenues. At street level there were shopping units while the large rooms above had been rented as offices by a number of organizations over the years. Many had been leased by the Imperial War Office during the First World War, when office space in Berlin had been at a premium. Commercial companies had come and gone as Germany's economic fortunes veered up and down throughout the 1920s and a Jewish company had used some parts of the building as recently as 1927. Above the door a black swastika in a white roundel indicated who the current tenants were. Just to make it clear to all passers-by, a large placard with a winged eagle carried the legend: 'Here only Nazis are required.' Above the placard, a long red, black and white banner draped all four upper floors. Berlin's Nazi Gauleiter or regional leader, Joseph Goebbels, had moved in two years before in 1928, when he chose to locate his administrative offices in the 25 rooms available at this imposing corner site. That particular evening, Goebbels was not working late at the office but was giving a speech in the Schöneberg district at the Sportpalast, his favourite arena in the city. Most of his guards were protecting him there and his base in Hedemannstrasse lay almost unprotected.

At 8.30 p.m. a group of fit, young uniformed men jumped down from a tram as it swung round to the left, opposite the corner doorway. Running towards the Gau HQ they quickly dragged the surprised SS guards into the building and out of public view. They then proceeded to beat them up – badly. Rushing up the stairs, they broke down the door to Goebbels' suite of offices and trashed them, kicking over chairs, tables and filing cabinets and scattering their contents. They did a professional job. Having made their mark, they left the building as quickly as they came, clutching bundles of files which they threw into the nearby Landwehr Canal, close to the spot where the body of the Marxist thinker and revolutionary Rosa Luxemburg had been dumped in the winter of 1919. They knew that the building would be lightly guarded that night and they took advantage of that piece of intelligence to send a stark message to Goebbels and his master Adolf Hitler. These thuggish vandals were not Jews, nor Reds nor any of the other groups that Hitler demonized in his speeches. They were loyal but disaffected and frustrated Nazis, the very men who had carried their leader ever closer to power for almost a decade. They were National Socialist stormtroopers, men of the SA.

The eclipse of the Brownshirts

In the late 1920s, the Nazi Party was in danger of splitting apart and many of the men in the SA legions were becoming dispirited. By 1929 they were over a million strong and their membership was continuing to grow as the Great Depression deepened. Their ranks were swollen by unemployed men who were desperate for radical social and economic change. For these men, it was the words Socialist and Workers in the Party's title, National Socialist German Workers' Party, that mattered. However, the Party leadership seemed to be moving in a different direction. The NSDAP's first policy programme, the 25 points published in 1920, had promised a socialistic approach to the economy: work guaranteed for all, the abolition of income based on 'rent-slavery', an expansion of existing old age welfare provision, the confiscation of wealth gained from war-profiteering, the nationalization of key industries, land reform in the public interest and a state committed to supporting small family businesses. But by the late 1920s, Hitler and the other key Party leaders seemed to be turning their backs on these communitarian principles. The public profile of the leaders was also changing. Hitler the street fighter was morphing into Hitler the socialite, travelling in his limousine and hobnobbing with the wealthy and privileged at the opera.

For almost a decade the SA had been doing the Nazi Party's political donkey work, campaigning relentlessly in local, state and national elections, recruiting new members, distributing propaganda, ruthlessly keeping the KPD on the back foot and off the streets and marching endlessly to maintain the sense of Party dynamism and purpose. Now they were in danger of becoming the forgotten wing of the Party, in the shadow of the new influential SS organizations that were preferred by the senior command. From the early days in Munich onwards, Hitler had always wanted to be protected by a small elite force that was completely dedicated to him, rather than to the Party at large and its wider ideals.

The first modest version of this unit, the *Saal-Schutz* or Hall Security, was specifically created to keep order in the beer halls while the leader was speaking. This group of bodyguards evolved through several formations and names: *Stabswache* (Staff Guard), *Stoßtrupp* (Shock Troop), *Schutzkommando* (Security Command) and *Sturmstaffel* (Storm Squad), before settling on *Schutzstaffel* (Security Squad). Under the highly competent and ambitious administrator Heinrich Himmler, the SS quickly developed into the most powerful, influential and well-disciplined organ of the NSDAP and later of the Nazi state. Unlike the rebel elements in the SA, the SS was more interested in Nazi ideology and racial theory than in dull economic matters. It was trusted by the three great Nazi potentates that were closest to Hitler by this stage: Goebbels, Göring and Himmler. By contrast, the SA increasingly seemed to be an amateur, semi-independent rabble that was over-radical and in danger of getting out of control.

The Stennes Revolt

The SA men who attacked the Berlin Gau offices were led by Walter Stennes. A highly decorated career soldier, after the Armistice Stennes took the well-worn path followed by many disillusioned, demobilized men by becoming a leader of a paramilitary Freikorps. By 1927 he was commander of the SA in Berlin and throughout eastern Germany. The immediate cause of his rebellious actions on 30 August 1930 was frustration. Men like Stennes had joined the NSDAP expecting revolution and they saw the SA as the core of a future revolutionary citizen-army. Now Stennes felt that the SA was being sidelined. Party financial resources were clearly being diverted to develop the SS or to high-profile projects that seemed like pointless flummery to men of action such as flags, uniforms, medals, parades and the rumoured extravagance of Hitler's pet project – the renovation of the Brown House in Munich. Hitler seemed to be distancing himself from the SA: he even refused to meet Stennes when he journeyed to

Munich to air his grievances in person. The SA action on Hedemannstrasse was not a plot against Hitler but a desperate ploy to gain his attention.

In the short term it seemed to have worked. A stunned Goebbels instantly relayed the news of the attack to Hitler and for good measure he added the embarrassing fact that the mutinous Stennes had refused to supply men to police his speech at the Sportpalast that evening. Hitler immediately made his apologies to his close friend Winifred Wagner, abandoned the Wagner Festival at Bayreuth and flew to Berlin at once. Both he and Goebbels, already wary of the turbulence simmering in SA ranks, feared that the Stennes insurrection might spread to other cities. The following day, Stennes sat down with the man who had snubbed him in Munich a few weeks before. Hitler was charming, concerned and amenable. He listened to Stennes' demands and met them. In front of 2,000 Berlin stormtroopers, the Führer admitted that he had been distracted by his many duties and had not paid enough attention to their grievances. He assured them that substantial new finances would be set aside for SA needs and that the Party would provide better legal support for men arrested by the police while carrying out operational duties. To ensure that the SA was better led, he would take personal command of the organization as its Supreme Leader. The relieved men in the crowd that evening bellowed out their oath of loyalty to the Führer. The revolution was back on, they believed.

Hitler took a different view of the affair. He had merely calmed the situation and bought time to think and prepare. Ever since the failed paramilitary Munich Putsch in 1923, Hitler had adopted a more cautious long-term strategy, looking to gain power through the ballot box rather than by depending upon violent action in the streets. His longer-term plans for German territorial expansion required the support of the nation's industrialists and its professional military. They would be his key allies in the future Reich that he was planning. The SA had been a useful tool in the early days of National Socialism but it now needed to be put in its place and more strictly controlled.

Suppressing SA dissent

Stennes believed that he had acted in the best interests of the NSDAP by pointing out the deep discontent within the SA. Hitler had seemed grateful to him for expressing his concerns but he was, of course, quietly furious. His first move was to recall his old friend and fellow warrior Ernst Röhm from self-imposed exile in Bolivia. Röhm was then appointed SA Führer, with a remit to make its regional officers such as Walter Stennes directly subordinate to Hitler and

Walter Stennes was one of the few Nazis to fall out with Hitler and live to tell the tale.

Röhm alone. Feeling betrayed, Stennes and his men rebelled again. Once more they sacked the Berlin Gau offices on Hedemannstrasse but this time they also rashly commandeered the offices of *Der Angriff*, the scurrilous daily newspaper edited by Goebbels. On 1 and 2 April they printed their own editions of the paper, explaining their actions and their feelings, but inevitably the Berlin SA was quickly purged and Stennes was expelled from the NSDAP. When the Nazi Reich came into being in 1933, Stennes and his family went into exile. Göring, who remembered Stennes' gallant war service, quietly advised him not to linger in Austria or Switzerland, a mistake that many refugees from the Nazis made at that time. He knew the depth of Hitler's anger and his capacity for patient revenge and had doubtless seen the death lists already being prepared by the SS. Stennes took the hint and was on the next boat to China, where he fought for Chiang Kai-shek against the communists until 1949.

At the same time, Hitler had been taking steps to eradicate the ideological roots of the dissension within the SA. The Strasser brothers, Gregor and Otto, were the standard-bearers for what some called 'social fascism'. They argued for the implementation of the broadly socialistic policies outlined in the NSDAP's founding programme, although the more radical Otto also held a distinctly different geopolitical world-view from Hitler. For Hitler, the ultimate enemy was the heart of Bolshevism, the Soviet Union. Otto believed instead that a future National Socialist German state should co-operate with the USSR against the greater foe: the Western capitalist states, which were under the sway of international Jewry. Important figures in the Party in the mid-1920s, when even Joseph Goebbels had supported them, the Strassers and their followers were now gradually marginalized. Hitler made it clear to both brothers that his opposition to them was based not just upon disagreements over Party policy but also personal antipathy.

Gregor Strasser then withdrew from politics altogether. Otto left the NSDAP in 1930 and established a breakaway Nazi group, the Combat League of Revolutionary National Socialists, which came to be known as the Black Front. Several hundred Berliner SA men joined the Black Front around the time of the second Stennes Revolt in April 1931 and the movement had more than 5,000 supporters by the time Hitler became Chancellor in January 1933. As Hitler then proceeded to isolate and control the various 'left-wing' nationalist groups in Germany, Otto moved first to Austria and then to Canada, via Czechoslovakia, France, Switzerland, Portugal and Bermuda. He had to keep moving as the Gestapo had put a price of half a million dollars on his head.

Nevertheless, on his travels he managed to found another anti-Hitler resistance group. In his time in Vienna and Prague he waged a continual propaganda war against Hitler and attempted to build an underground network of dissident Brownshirts within the Third Reich.

Decapitating the SA

The problem of the SA continued to rumble on throughout the first 16 months of Hitler's time as Chancellor. Germany's industrial and commercial leaders had now been convinced that Hitler was 'good for business' but they feared the persistent talk of a 'second revolution' in SA circles. Ernst Röhm continued to make occasional Strasserist remarks, exhorting his old comrade Hitler to finish the job that he had set out to do in 1920. The strength of the SA also concerned the leadership elite of the German army. The Reichswehr was still pinned to a maximum number of 100,000 men by the 1919 Versailles Settlement. Versailles also laid down strict regulations on the size of the army's officer cadre as well as imposing restrictions on the German manufacture or import of specific types of weaponry and munitions. On the other hand, in 1933 more than three million men were available to Röhm and the other hotheads that were in charge of the SA. And both Goebbels and Himmler were now reporting that the presence of so many loutish and intimidating young men on the streets of Germany was being questioned by the citizenry. Was there really a need for so many aggressive Brownshirts now that Hitler was in power? Hitler understood and increasingly agreed with these sentiments.

The necessary wheels were put in motion, but administrative proposals in early 1934 to clip Röhm's wings and bring the SA under tighter central control generated bad feeling between Hitler and his old friend. Himmler and the rising star of the SS, Reinhard Heydrich, had compiled a dossier full of dirt that revealed the extent of Röhm's financial and sexual corruption and were happy to pass it over to the rather puritanical Führer. They got a green light from Hitler to go ahead and draw up lists of targets while the army was quietly put on full alert. Hitler phoned Röhm's adjutant himself and told him that he would be spending the weekend in Bavaria and wanted to meet the SA regional leadership that Saturday morning. The meeting was scheduled for 11 a.m. on 30 June at the pretty town of Bad Wiessee, on the western shore of Lake Tegernsee in the Bavarian Alps.

By 6 a.m. that morning, most of the SA leadership in Munich had been rounded up and were in prison. Hitler then led an SS convoy to Bad Wiessee and by 7 a.m. the houses and hotels containing the SA leadership had been sealed off. The Führer then personally confronted and arrested Röhm. The SA Gauleiter for Breslau and his catamite were dragged from their bed and shot through the head in the hotel garden. As SA leaders from other parts of Germany arrived for their meeting later that day, they were met on the platform of Bad Wiessee Bahnhof by heavily armed SS detachments and taken away to their fate.

Röhm was detained at Stadelheim Prison in Munich for 36 hours, protesting his loyalty and awaiting his fate. Out of respect for his position in the Party, he received a generous offer from his old pal Hitler, conveyed by the SS. For his years of service, he was awarded the privilege of doing away with himself. When he refused, he was instantly executed. Gregor Strasser was also shot, although he had left politics altogether and resumed his career as a chemist more than a year before. Across Germany, armed Gestapo and SS units were busy wiping out other possible sources of resistance to Hitler.

The Chancellor himself almost became one of the many Nazi casualties that morning. As his cavalcade prepared to return to Munich, a truck full of heavily armed SA men arrived at the hotel where Röhm had been staying. In the confusion of the moment, and distressed on learning that their leaders had been shot or arrested, the SA men prepared for combat with the SS men in the hotel forecourt. Hitler intervened and only just managed to convince the disgruntled SA men to get back on their truck and return to Munich. As they left Bad Wiessee, however, they decided to turn the tables on Hitler by liquidating his SS guard, killing him and liberating their imprisoned leaders. They hid their truck in the trees outside the village, set up an ambush that included two heavy machine guns and waited for Hitler's car to come speeding around the corner and into their trap. Only Hitler's natural wariness and deep sense of survival saved him that morning. Suspicious of the SA detachment's attitude, he ordered his driver to take an alternative route back to the city. It would not be the last time that a sudden decision to change his plans would save Adolf Hitler's life.

Street fighting man Ernst Röhm was leader of the Sturmabteilung, *which specialized in beer hall brawls. By 1934 he had come to expect the rewards that came with power, but Hitler gave him more than he had bargained for.*

CHAPTER 7

1933–38
Resistance in the New Germany

A dolf and Anton had much in common. They were both native Austrians who chose to fight in the Imperial German Army during the First World War. Both acquired German citizenship at a later stage in life, both were right-wing nationalists who detested socialists and communists and both were fervent anti-Semites. And the pair of them inspired the young intellectual Joseph Goebbels. In the early 1920s both men spent time in Landsberg Prison as a result of their political crimes and they both inhabited cell no. 7 on the second floor, though at different times. There was much for each man to admire in the other's beliefs and actions, but they came from different social backgrounds and were separated by one bitter political chasm. Adolf came from a petit bourgeois background whereas Anton was an aristocrat who came from an exceptionally rich family that owned estates in Austria, Germany and Italy. Each of Anton's parents had brought immense wealth to their marriage and his uncle was the great English historian and linguist Lord Acton. The family's ancestral home was the stunning Castello di Arco, which sits on a high mountain spur looking south towards the tip of Lake Garda. Anton's full name told his story by itself: Anton von Padua Alfred Emil Hubert Georg Graf von Arco auf Valley.

Murder by aristocrat

After serving in the last year of the war, the young Arco-Valley found himself in the chaos of post-war Munich, where he planned to enrol in the university. He was quickly sucked into the maelstrom of Bavarian politics. Anton Arco-Valley particularly despised Kurt Eisner, the Jewish socialist writer who had engineered the collapse of the Bavarian monarchy in November 1918 and was now prime minister of the new People's State of Bavaria. He expressed his contempt for Eisner by gunning him down in public in Munich on 21 February 1919. Eisner was on his way to the opening session of the newly elected Bavarian Parliament when Arco-Valley stepped out from a doorway and fired at his head and his back at short range. The murder sparked off several days of street warfare and a cycle of reprisal killings.

Arco-Valley made no attempt to escape from Munich or to hide the fact that he was the assassin. In any case, Eisner's bodyguard had fired several return shots, wounding Arco-Valley in the head, the chest and the spine. These injuries and his sudden notoriety and popularity among the nationalists and monarchists across Bavaria would have made both flight or subterfuge impossible and unnecessary. Many considered him a heroic and patriotic son of Bavaria for murdering the Bolshevik Jew. Thanks to a sympathetic conservative judge, Arco-Valley avoided the gallows and was sent to the relatively comfortable Landsberg Prison for five years.

All must hold their tongues

After his release in 1925 he undertook a number of propaganda duties for monarchist and federalist groupings in Bavaria. He believed that the old Wittelsbach dynasty should be restored and hoped that Bavaria would recover the semi-independence from the Germanic capitals of Vienna and Berlin that it had enjoyed in the past. This brought him into serious conflict with Hitler, who had no time for the old historic chequerboard of small principalities and imperial free cities that in his view had weakened Germany for centuries. Hitler's vision was of one strong, unified national state that contained all the ethnic Germans living in central and eastern Europe within its borders. In his Munich beer hall days, he had been as keen to disrupt the meetings of 'separatist' monarchists as to burst into communist ones. Arco-Valley would also fall foul of the Nazis in other ways.

Like many in his social class, he was known to make disparaging comments about 'the little corporal' and he continued to repeat these remarks publicly after Hitler became Chancellor in January 1933. He had also been heard to make a much more dangerous statement: he had said that he would be happy and willing to commit another political assassination if it were necessary. In the eyes of the SS and the Gestapo, the presumed target of this boast could only be Hitler. Arco-Valley quickly found himself under observation and then in custody.

Anton von Padua Alfred Emil Hubert Georg Graf von Arco auf Valley, to give him his full name, was born with a silver spoon in his mouth, but that didn't stop him from getting sucked into reactionary politics.

There he was persuaded to give the new authorities his assurance that he would refrain from insulting or assaulting the new Führer or any other leading Nazi in any way. In the circumstances, Anton agreed. As a nobleman, he was bound to keep his word and was therefore quickly released, but he remained under discreet surveillance. He behaved circumspectly throughout the Nazi years and in 1941 the technical death sentence that had been passed upon him in 1920 for the Eisner murder was scratched from the Munich court records. In reality Arco-Valley was an unlikely assassin. He almost certainly never considered a detailed plan to murder Hitler, but his arrest and examination by the Nazi authorities sent a very clear message to the old upper classes that even a privileged tongue had to be kept under control in the New Germany.

Policed by abbreviations

Once the new Third Reich was fully established, its citizens found themselves monitored and policed by a collection of changing abbreviations and initials. From 1936 onwards, everyday police work to maintain civic safety, plus the emergency organizations such as the coastguard and the fire service, were the responsibilities of the Ordnungspolizei, known as the Orpo. Purely criminal detective investigations that had no security implications were in the hands of the Kriminalpolizei or Kripo. Since 1931 the *Sicherheitsdienst* or SD had acted as the intelligence service of the Nazi Party and the SS, but under Himmler and his assistant Heydrich it acquired ever greater powers of supervision over the population. By 1936 Himmler also controlled the *Geheime Staatspolizei* or Gestapo, an arrangement that was meant to encourage more effective co-operation between the organs of the state and the Party. A major reform in 1939 put most of the nation's security and police agencies under one umbrella, the RSHA or Reich Main Security Office.

Contrary to the image presented by Hollywood of an all-seeing, all-knowing and ruthlessly efficient network of agents and spies, the German police and security framework in the Third Reich muddled through like all such organizations throughout history. It suffered from the same issues of jurisdiction overlap, poor inter-communication, personal and departmental rivalries and misallocation of resources that afflict all complex government systems. A lack of experienced manpower was common to all of the above bodies and that problem only increased after 1940 as trained officers found themselves diverted towards the war effort, often into *Waffen* or armed units such as the battalions of Orpo men who found themselves performing lower-level military tasks in occupied eastern Europe. Within the Reich, the Gestapo never had enough resources to deal with the overabundance of information that came its way. From its foundation in Prussia in 1933, it was swamped by a continual flood of complaints and suspicions offered up by loyal citizens of the Reich, who suspected their neighbours or even close family members of treasonable acts. It took valuable time and energy to winnow through the paperwork in order to discard the many denunciations that were fuelled by local disputes or marital malice and find the nuggets of real evidence.

Hitler's own personal security arrangements exemplified the problem with the German government during the Third Reich. At different times, in different places and at different types of events, he was protected by numerous agencies – the Führer Schutzkommando FSK, the Führer Begleitbattalion FBB, the Führer Begleitkommando FBK and the Leibstandarte SS Adolf Hitler LSSAH – all with conflicting and overlapping responsibilities. On at least one occasion, the lack of communication between these bodies led to Hitler arriving at an almost empty railway platform accompanied only by an adjutant, a secretary and a chauffeur. In another instance, Hitler's chauffeur slammed the pedal to the ground when he realized that a gang of armed men in a black saloon car had appeared from nowhere and were closing at speed. However, they were merely an official escort that had joined the road from a hidden layby when the Führer's car entered their sector of responsibility.

Resistance cells

Nor were the Nazi authorities as ruthless and efficient as they hoped when it came to finding and destroying oppositionist groups, although they got better at it over time. Walter Loewenheim was well known to the Nazis long before they came to power. An active member of several leftist groups throughout the 1920s including the Spartakists, the Free Socialists and the KPD, he eventually left the communists in 1927, protesting at their reluctance to mobilize the German working class against the Nazis and other fascistic parties in Germany. Desperate to provoke a more militant reaction to the Nazis, he founded an underground cell, Circle 29, which was later known as the Leninist Organization. Loewenheim hoped that this would be the foundation for a network of German socialist leaders who would be ready to take advantage of the inevitable collapse of Hitlerism predicted by Marxist theorists. In October 1933 his programme for action, *New Beginnings*, was published in Prague and illegally smuggled into Germany for distribution to workers in key industries.

Hitler cuts a solitary figure as he hits the road again on another exhausting trip to meet his adoring public.

By late 1934, Loewenheim's group may have had as many as 500 members, until like many other leftist groups it dissolved in a factional row.

By that time, all democratic parties on the left such as the Social Democrats had long since been disbanded or dissolved. Those KPD members who had not yet perished in the camps were either still languishing there or in many cases had re-invented themselves as Beefsteak Nazis, those much derided latecomers to the ranks of the SA who were brown on the outside but red inside. Nevertheless, Loewenheim continued to publish and distribute broadsheets and pamphlets that reached factory workers in most industrial German cities. He only left Germany in September 1935, partly because his underground activities were having little impact and also because he had begun to feel the Gestapo breathing down his neck.

A fan of Stalin

Although the Gestapo eventually arrested the subversive Ernst Niekisch in 1937, the Nazi authorities dealt with him in a relatively lenient way by their standards. Perhaps that was because there were elements in Niekisch's political thinking that chimed with Nazism. He was a proud German nationalist and was hostile to the Versailles Settlement which had left Germany humiliated, militarily weak and stripped of much of its borderlands. Also, he was anti-Semitic and anti-democratic and some of his remarks against 'international Jewish capitalism' could have come from the Nazis' weekly anti-Jewish tabloid, *Der Stürmer*. Like the Nazis, Neikisch also believed that Germany needed a strong leader with dictatorial powers. However, his support and admiration was offered to Josef Stalin rather than Adolf Hitler.

In early post-war Munich he had initially supported Eisner and then the Social Democrats, not Hitler and his Nazis. Like some of those on the 'left wing' of the Nazi Party such as the Strasser brothers, he argued that Germany should co-operate with the Soviet Union against the corrupt and failing Western democracies. Moreover, he thought Hitler was a vulgar demagogue and that the concentration of all power in his hands, the so-called Führer Principle, was a shallow foundation for building a better Germany.

By contrast, Niekisch praised Soviet collective planning and Stalin's Five-Year Plans, which seemed to be building a powerful economy in the 1930s. Rather than National Socialism, he called his particular political recipe National Bolshevism. At a personal level, he deeply disliked Hitler and a meeting with his former friend and supporter Goebbels almost ended in a brawl. Niekisch made no secret of his opinions: in 1926 he became a member of the Old Socialists party, he published the anti-Nazi newspaper *Widerstand* or 'Resistance' until December 1934 and he continued to distribute his 1932 pamphlet 'Hitler – a German disaster' long after the establishment of the Third Reich. When he was finally charged with high treason, he was sentenced to life imprisonment. He was lucky. Others had been executed for much less in the purges of 1933 and 1934. Over 1,100 'Old Socialists' were arrested by the Gestapo in 1935 alone, but Niekisch enjoyed a few more years of freedom than most. One rumour suggested that he had friends in high Nazi places thanks to his boyhood in the Bavarian town of Nördlingen, while others said that the over-worked Gestapo had just forgotten about him. He finally emerged from prison in 1945.

The Grunow mystery

There was a great deal of luck in the survival or otherwise of underground resistance groups in the 1930s. The members of the Markwitz Circle, a small Social Democrat resistance group, certainly discussed their desire to eliminate Hitler and gave some thought to the mechanics of assassinating such a well-protected target. However, the group spent most of its time distributing oppositionist literature, which it stored in the pub where it held its meetings, so it was very quickly detected and infiltrated by the Gestapo. Around a dozen group members were sentenced to life imprisonment. By contrast, the ex-Nazi agent Heinrich Grunow sustained his resistance campaign against Hitler for almost a decade. Grunow left the NSDAP in 1932 after coming into contact with Otto Strasser and joining his Black Front. He was rounded up in the summer of 1933 when the Nazis undertook their first big sweep against the socialists and communists. Fortunately, he was considered to be a minor threat and spent only two months in a 're-education' camp. Once released he teamed up with Otto Strasser in Prague.

In his book *Flight from Terror*, published by the New York Book Club in 1943, Strasser told a compelling tale of Grunow's contribution to the fight against fascism. Grunow apparently approached Strasser in 1935 claiming to be a member of Hitler's bodyguard at the Berghof, then something of a building site as Hitler's modest chalet was being transformed into an imperial complex. Grunow was determined to kill Hitler in revenge for the murder of his friend and mentor Ernst Röhm the previous summer. His plan involved the new road that was being built up to the Berghof. Cars had to slow down at one half-completed stretch where a tight curve was bordered by a stand of pines, so it

German dissident and former Nazi Party member Otto Strasser addresses members of the Black Front at Burg Lauenburg, Saxony, 1932.

was the perfect spot for a rifleman. Strasser encouraged Grunow and assured him that the Black Front would support him in any way possible. Two days later he received a call that confirmed that Grunow had immediately returned to the Reich and successfully carried out his task.

Grunow had waited at night near the wooded bend in the road, his eyes following the distant headlights snaking up the hill and lurching from side to side at every corner on the road, signalling the approach of the Führer's Mercedes. He could hear the gears crunch down as the vehicle arrived at the stretch of unfinished surface. The limousine was close enough for Grunow to see that there were only two men in the car, Hitler and his chauffeur Julius Schreck. Both could be easily made out in the Alpine moonlight, so Grunow levelled his rifle and dealt with his target. The figure in the front passenger seat shuddered and tried to lift himself out of his seat, clawing the air and howling his last. He had got his man, he thought. His trim 'snot-brush' moustache was clearly visible. The Führer slumped back in his seat while the chauffeur squashed the pedal and skidded at speed away from the rough-gravelled trap. Now that his mission was completed and knowing what his future held if he fell into Nazi hands, Grunow withdrew a revolver from his jacket, shoved the muzzle in his mouth and pulled the trigger. He would never discover that his undertaking was a failure and that his death was in vain.

Strasser explained all. Earlier that evening back in Munich, Schreck had been suffering from a badly infected tooth and a painful jaw and the car-loving Führer had been happy to change places with his old pal. The moustache Grunow had seen had been Schreck's, who had styled it like Hitler's as a sign of the deep friendship between the two old comrades; and also, it was rumoured, because Schreck often acted as Hitler's double. In his book, Strasser told the story of the moonlight killing with dramatic vigour and tragic irony. But Strasser was a larger-than-life character and a great raconteur who revelled in telling and exaggerating the tales that he shared with his pals around the table or at the bar. Once safely in Great Britain or in the USA, many Nazis made some cash selling their reminiscences of life in the Reich. Most were guilty of the sins of exaggeration and omission and they were all keen to ensure that it was their version of events that was remembered. Strasser in particular knew how to create a story in a way that would attract the attention of a publisher and keep his readers turning the page.

In fact, Heinrich Grunow's real adventures needed no elaboration. After he was released from the camps in 1933, Grunow spent the next seven years working as a secret courier for several anti-Nazi organizations. By 1936 the Nazi authorities had changed their minds about his harmlessness and attempted to kidnap him by luring him to a meeting at Zinnwald near the Czech–German frontier. Although Grunow was badly beaten up at the rendezvous, the operation was botched. He escaped and carried on his work among the ever-growing émigré community in Paris. In autumn 1939 he discussed the feasibility of plans to kill Hitler with the French military intelligence agency the Deuxième Bureau. This leaked back to Berlin and the Reich Main Security Office placed Grunow on the list of dangerous public enemies to be arrested in the event of a successful invasion of France. For good measure, he was also added to the list of individuals to be rounded up by the SS once the Wehrmacht had occupied the British Isles. The Gestapo finally seized him in Paris in the aftermath of the Fall of France in spring 1940 and he died, or was killed, in Sachsenhausen concentration camp in March 1945. By then, the security organs of the Third Reich had had much more practice at catching and disposing of their enemies.

CHAPTER 8

1935–38

Implausible Plots

The young man in the train compartment could hear and feel the train slowing. Then the sudden convergence of a dozen or more separate iron tracks into one parallel mass confirmed that he was almost at Nuremberg railway station. His ticket for the journey from Prague to Stuttgart, where he had lived until the year before, was dated 20 December 1936. A new law meant that students of his religion could no longer enrol in German universities and so he had gone to study in Czechoslovakia. Although his close family had soon joined him in exile, he still had relatives and friends in Stuttgart and therefore had a reason for travelling there. However, he was intending to cut his journey short and get off the train at Nuremberg. His instructions were simple, clear and had been hammered into his memory by Heinrich Grunow, his handler from the Black Front back in Prague.

A single room had been booked for him in a small, typically nondescript 'railway hotel' on the other side of the tram tracks that ran across the Bahnhofplatz. Once he'd checked in, he was instructed to go out again for a stroll along Nuremberg's impressive medieval walls. At some point, he would bump into a Black Front contact who would slip two small paper tickets into his hand. These could be exchanged at the baggage window in the station for two suitcases, which had possibly followed a circuitous route to Nuremberg via the densely wooded hills that ran along much of the Czech–German border. They contained explosives.

Once he had collected his two items of baggage, the young man was free to start thinking how best to use them. His handler well understood the difficulties of carrying out clandestine action on enemy territory. There were always too many unforeseen risks and unexpected obstacles to stick to a rigid plan. However, the young Jewish volunteer terrorist was an intelligent and capable 20-year-old and German was his native tongue. He seemed deeply committed to carrying out an attack of some kind that would shake the Nazis, in a town that Hitler called 'our beautiful and historic Parade City'. Grunow had therefore not given him a specific target but had left it to the young Helmut Hirsch to make his own judgement about what he could achieve on the day.

Grunow had, however, suggested two targets that might be suitable for the young man's luggage bombs. The first was the regional Nazi HQ or Gau Haus on Marienplatz, now renamed Schlageter Platz after one of the SA 'martyrs' who had fallen at Hitler's side in the 1923 Putsch. It was a busy office block but lightly guarded. Another possible target was the building where Julius Streicher churned out his savagely anti-Semitic newspaper *Der Stürmer*. Again, this was also very lightly guarded. After all, Nazi institutions had few enemies in Nuremberg in 1935. And if Hirsch got lucky, he might just get close to the biggest target of them all.

Every year on 24 December, Hitler met with his oldest supporters at a special Christmas Eve gathering in Munich. He was known to enjoy stopping over in Nuremberg en route to Bavaria from Berlin, usually staying at the Deutscher Hof Hotel. From his balcony, which bore the words 'HEIL HITLER' spelled out in giant Christmas lights, the Führer could look out across the loveliest of German cities bedecked in its festive garb, amidst the usual panoply of giant swastika flags. Hitler had last been in Nuremberg on 8 December but had then gone north to the capital for a series of meetings with the Polish and British ambassadors. It was very likely that he would stop over at Nuremberg on his way back south to his Christmas party in Munich, so Hirsch and Hitler would be in the city at the same time. A successful attack on the Führer seemed unlikely but, Grunow shrugged, assassins do sometimes get lucky, as Gavrilo Princip discovered in 1914. Failing all these possibilities, Hirsch could take his suitcases to the Nazi Party rally ground just outside the city and see what damage he could inflict on the symbolic buildings there.

Second thoughts

That was the vague plan. Unfortunately, at Nuremberg railway station Hirsch began to reflect on his position. The five-hour journey had given him time to think about the risks he was taking. It was one thing to sit in a Prague bar with fellow plotters and volunteer for action but it was a very different thing to be alone in the heart of the Nazi Reich. Hirsch had been dismayed by the long delay at the German border and the very thorough way in which the guards had examined the paperwork and the travel plans of everyone crossing the frontier. He had easily convinced his parents that he was going skiing with friends for a couple of days in the hills north of Prague, but had the border guards who questioned him actually been convinced by his cover story? He had told them that he was returning to Stuttgart to see his mother, who was ill.

In fact, the Gestapo already knew that the entire Hirsch family were living together in Prague by that point in time. The Black Front had been penetrated by at least one double agent and the Gestapo knew about Hirsch's link to the Front. They must have watched him on the train, perhaps noticing the rising tension as his resolve evaporated. Hirsch decided to stay on the train at Nuremberg and never met up with his contact or the suitcases. Instead, he travelled all the way to Stuttgart, hoping to meet an old school friend and discuss what he should do next. Late that night he took a room at the Hotel Pelikan, another nondescript railway hotel. It was there that the Gestapo arrested him at just after midnight on 21 December. Neither the contact nor the explosives made it far into Germany, as they both quickly fell into the hands of the Gestapo.

After many weeks of solitary imprisonment and 'questioning', Hirsch was tried for high treason. Technically he was a still a German citizen, if an unwelcome one in the eyes of the Nazi regime. The secondary charge was possession of explosives in order to commit a criminal act, though it's almost certain that he carried no weapon of any kind during his brief return to Germany. In addition, he was charged with intending to assassinate the Führer. When he was asked to confirm this, the young student bravely but unwisely stated that he very much wanted to kill Hitler. His honest answer gained him attention in the foreign press and also won him a little time as a result.

Hirsch's father Siegfried had worked in the USA before 1914 and had US citizenship, so Helmut therefore claimed and won American citizenship, although he had never been in the USA. The case now had an international dimension, with US and European newspapers, politicians and diplomats all playing a part in a vigorous campaign for his release. The League of Nations and the International Red Cross appealed on his behalf while Norway offered to give him asylum and vouch for his future good behaviour. Hitler was unmoved. Helmut Hirsch was beheaded at the House of Death in Plötzensee Prison on 4 June 1937.

A fractured opposition

Hirsch was truly an innocent abroad. His only crime was his desire to show the world that Jews were not just passive victims but were capable of taking a stand against their Nazi oppressors. However, his experience revealed that by the mid-1930s the Gestapo had developed more effective systems and procedures and that its intelligence gathering and monitoring abilities extended beyond the borders of the Reich. Hirsch had been followed by German agents from the moment he hugged his parents goodbye in Prague and set out on his pointless quest.

Other plans to disrupt the Nazi regime and strike at its leadership in the years between 1935 and 1939 were equally futile. The plotters were often acting alone, or at most in a very small group, with little real organizational support. What is more, the activists involved almost always lacked the military or technical background to avoid the attention of the German security organizations and get close to a meaningful Nazi target: few had any training in fieldcraft. Attempts to get near enough to a leading figure such as Hitler became increasingly desperate as the ring of security around the Führer became more professional. The sources of dissent that could have posed an organized threat to the Nazi regime were paralysed.

The speedy imposition of a totalitarian state in 1933 had decapitated and demoralized the Social Democrats and the KPD and the remaining underground vestiges of these parties failed to co-operate against their common enemy. The SPD had always distrusted the anti-democratic communists, who assumed, as suggested by the Marxist interpretation of history, that Hitlerism was a temporary phenomenon and was inevitably bound to disintegrate quite quickly as a result of its internal contradictions. Besides, the remaining communists within Germany followed instructions from their masters in Moscow. Those German KPD leaders who escaped to the Soviet Union in the first year or so of the new Reich were soon out of touch with the realities inside Germany. And Stalin was slow to appreciate just how bellicose Hitler really was. He expected that Russia and Germany would eventually come to some kind of geopolitical understanding, so the KPD remnants left behind in Germany were not encouraged to rock the boat. It was left to individuals and very small groups to try and destabilize the Nazi leadership.

Killings in Davos and Paris

The case of David Frankfurter, another potential assassin who was Jewish, shows how difficult it was for lone wolves to get close to their top enemies. Frankfurter was a medical student who left Germany in 1933 to live in Switzerland. His frequent return visits to the Reich to contact friends and family made him very aware of how conditions of daily life for German Jews were deteriorating. Like Hirsch, Frankfurter wanted to make a statement of Jewish defiance but from the outset he realized that he had no expectation of success if he was too ambitious. He had given some thought to assassinating Hitler but quickly admitted to himself that killing a top Nazi in Germany was almost impossible, so he settled for doing something about the rising tide of Nazism in his adopted home.

After practising how to fire a pistol, he set out to assassinate Wilhelm Gustloff, a German citizen who had founded an NSDAP foreign section to promote Nazi values and activities in Switzerland. On 4 February 1936 Frankfurter presented himself at Gustloff's home in Davos in eastern Switzerland, shot him in the head and torso several times and then handed himself in to the local authorities. The Nazis made Gustloff into a racial martyr, proclaiming that his murder was further evidence of the Jewish global conspiracy to subvert the Aryan Race. Gustloff enjoyed a lavish state funeral in his home town of Schwerin, attended by the entire Nazi top brass, and Germany put immense diplomatic pressure on the Swiss, who were criticized for harbouring Jews and other anti-Nazi dissidents. Bern fortunately ignored the outcry in the German press for the killer to be deported back to the Reich and face his punishment there. The Swiss sentenced Frankfurter to 18 years in prison which almost certainly saved his life. He was released in 1945, four weeks after the death of Hitler.

Frankfurter had hoped that his act would at least inspire other Jews to turn on their oppressors and possibly even spark them into planning an organized insurgency against Nazism. There was no general uprising, but one 17-year-old Polish-Jewish student eventually followed in Frankfurter's steps. On 7 November 1938, Herschel Grynszpan walked into the German Embassy in Paris claiming to be a German citizen with important confidential information for the ambassador. However, His Excellency Count von Welczeck had, in fact, just left the building, passing Grynszpan in the hallway. His ambitious assassin had not recognized him and therefore had to settle for smaller fry in the shape of a junior diplomatic official, Ernst vom Rath, who took five bullets in his lower torso. Grynszpan's victim struggled for life for the next two days, unsuccessfully attended by the best surgeons in Paris and by Karl Brandt, Hitler's favourite doctor of the moment. Vom Rath's death gave the Nazis another opportunity to do 'something positive' about the Jewish Threat. The Kristallnacht pogrom, the night of broken glass, took place on the night of 9–10 November 1938, the

David Frankfurter had given some thought to putting an end to Adolf Hitler, but finally opted to kill Wilhelm Gustloff.

anniversary of the 1923 Munich Beer Hall Putsch, a few hours after Hitler was informed of vom Rath's death.

Fake SS

If Hitler was too well protected by his SS bodyguards, then why not infiltrate the SS and replace Hitler loyalists with oppositionists? That was the logical solution to 'the Hitler problem' that occurred to Dr Helmut Mylius in 1934. Mylius was a successful businessman with industrial interests and his own publishing concern. His politics were conservative and he headed up a small organization that advocated more support for private enterprise and smaller-scale businesses. But he didn't care much for government by Hitler and the Nazis. They seemed too engaged with ideological issues rather than the practical running of the German economy. At some point in late 1934 Mylius came into contact with a much more colourful character, who shared some of his views about the new government.

Captain Hermann Ehrhardt was a veteran of the Battle of Jutland and had been a 'guest' of the Royal Navy at Scapa Flow at the end of the First World War. A prominent figure in Germany during the years of post-war chaos, he commanded his own Freikorps brigade of over 6,000 men, many of them ex-naval monarchist officers like himself. With the connivance of Munich's police chief Ernst Pöhner he ran the Bavarian Wood Products Company. This was a front for Organization Consul, a terrorist assassination squad that had cells operating throughout Germany by 1922. By the end of that year, the OC had morphed into a more public organization, the Viking League, that was akin to Hitler's SA.

Ehrhardt's star waned in 1923, as Hitler came to dominate radical right-wing politics in southern Germany. Many of his men defected to Hitler's ranks and Ehrhardt was marginalized. Attempts to link the remnants of his group with dissident National Socialists such as the Strasser brothers and Walter Stennes consumed much of his time but came to nothing. In early June 1934, Ehrhardt suddenly took a trip to Austria and didn't come back. It's likely that one of his old comrades who had deserted him for Hitler had had the decency to let him know that he was on the list of men to be liquidated in the Long Knives purge.

Two unlikely partners in crime, Dr Mylius and Captain Ehrhardt had one thing in common: a dislike of the Nazis. The street gossip that eventually reached Gestapo ears was that the two were planning to infiltrate the SS with men that they, and not Hitler, could rely on. More likely, Ehrhardt was hoping to make contact with some of his former men who were now in the SS and play upon old friendships and shared memories. It was also rumoured that as many as 160 SS members who were formerly Ehrhardt's men were ready to obey their old commander. Mylius's role was probably to fund the necessary travel and expenses. Like many other other whispered plots of the period, though, it was based on a fantasy.

The men whom Hitler chose to protect him were fanatical National Socialists and were bound to him by a deep sense of loyalty and personal honour. As the old trusted warriors from the early days in Munich were promoted or grew old and fat, they were replaced by young believers. For many of them, Hitler was not just a political leader but a messianic father figure. Their personal attachment to Hitler was marked by the change in the name of their unit from SS-Sonderkommando Berlin to the more emotionally binding Leibstandarte SS Adolf Hitler, the Führer's own Lifeguard. These were men who carried out his orders in the June 1934 purge without question or hesitation, whether gunning down senior army officers or long-standing heroes of the Party. At a point in history when Germany was resurgent under Hitler's leadership, the idea that these men would desert the Führer's side for a largely forgotten name from the past was simply not credible. The Mylius–Ehrhardt plot may in fact have simply been little more than wishful musings muttered after a long night on the schnapps. Nevertheless, Ehrhardt fled and Mylius wisely used his connection with Field Marshal Erich von Manstein to get a useful administrative post in the supply and logistics side of the Wehrmacht. There he could demonstrate his loyalty to his country and get the Gestapo off his back.

A message from Mussolini

Ten assassins. Ten suicide bombers. All former officers in the Prussian police. Each one was arrested by the Nazis and sent to a re-education camp as a punishment for their conscientious service to the Weimar Republic. Ten men with ruined careers, bursting with anger and looking for revenge. Camp officials would need to be bribed to speed up the release of these prisoners into civil society. Then they would be given training and a new identity as couriers in the Italian army and the Italian diplomatic service. As uniformed officials of Germany's closest ally, they would be ushered into the very heart of the Nazi web without raising too much suspicion. A small but highly explosive device would be sewn into their stylish Italian uniforms, adorned with fascist insignia, and each man was targeted upon a member of the Third Reich's ruling cabinet, from the monster Hitler downwards. As they delivered their special letters from Rome to each of their individual targets, they would detonate the devices and wipe out the senior echelon of the Nazi state. Pulling the strings behind these ten brave freedom-fighters was a mysterious *éminence grise* dedicated to restoring freedom to Germany.

An interesting plot for a movie perhaps, but unlikely to play well in the tense city gearing up for war that was Berlin in the late summer of 1938. The wily puppet master was said to be Wilhelm Abegg, a Prussian government official of great ability and dedication. There were many reasons why the Nazis disliked Abegg. He was not only an intellectual but he was also a left-leaning moderate with a Jewish wife. Added to that, he had rooted out corrupt and lazy officials in the Prussian police service and at a critical moment in German history in the early 1920s he had promoted senior police officials who were committed to the new Weimar democracy and the rule of law. He also monitored the Nazis and created interesting dossiers, especially on Hitler's reliance upon his big industrial donors.

Unsurprisingly, Abegg and his family left Germany for Switzerland early in 1933. The Nazis were always going to throw mud at him once he was removed from office and the Italian courier plot may have been their invention. It not only tarred Abegg as a dishonourable traitor but it was meant to humiliate him in the eyes of the German public. Who else but one of those unreliable and otherworldly socialist eggheads could have devised such an impracticable and absurd proposal? Sadly, Wilhelm Abegg was never a convincing assassin. However, Berlin was full or rumours that other plots with a better chance of success were in the offing.

Rumour or humour?

The Sportpalast was a giant indoor stadium for winter sports in the Schöneberg district of Berlin, south of the Tiergarten. When it opened in 1910 it was an architectural wonder. It was the largest roofed arena in Germany and the largest ice rink for skating and ice hockey in the world. In addition to international skating competitions, it hosted the notorious and gruelling six-day bicycle marathons that transfixed the sporting public of Weimar Berlin. And Max Schmeling, heavyweight boxing champion of the world from 1930 to 1932, fought his way up the ranks in the Sportpalast in the late 1920s. Behind the podium used for speeches by all kinds of associations and political parties, there was a giant cinema screen. The steeply raked galleries meant that everyone in the 14,000-strong crowd could see and hear perfectly. Once the Nazis came to power, the microphones and loudspeakers were quickly upgraded so that every syllable uttered by Hitler and Goebbels would carry through the auditorium. When Hitler spoke in the arena, giant banners spelled out the party slogan of the month: 'Marxism must be destroyed', 'The Jews are our bad luck', 'Germany needs colonies', 'Total war is the shortest war', 'The Führer commands and we follow'. Goebbels particularly liked the acoustics in the hall which helped create an ecstatic, frenzied atmosphere. In the first few years of the Third Reich, smart promoters even cashed in on the brief enthusiasm in Berlin for all things Teutonic and put on evenings of Bavarian oompah music, with beer and bockwurst brought to the tables by suitably dirndled Aryan maidens.

And at one point in 1937 an unknown German soldier apparently found himself locked in a toilet at the Sportpalast. That afternoon he had planted a bomb under the speaker's platform, but before setting the timer he needed to attend to another more pressing matter. The bomb could wait, he thought: Hitler had a reputation for orating at great length. But the soldier never got back in time to activate the device. Curiously, a trained soldier with skills in detonating explosives was unable to master the lock on a jammed toilet door. Hitler arrived at the podium and left it unscathed two hours later. The fate of the trapped soldier remains unknown, just like every other missing detail in this unlikely tale.

The story seems to have circulated as a rumour in Berlin and in other cities where it was still sometimes possible to make a joke that related to the Nazis. The current author first heard this tale in the 1970s, when it was mentioned by a number of German citizens who had been sent to Britain after the war to assist in reconstruction work. They knew the story but dismissed it as one of the many jokes that quietly did the rounds among trusted friends when they were sure there were no Nazi snoops around. The punchline suggested that the trapped soldier had at least spent the evening with his own ordure, while the audience at the Sportpalast had had to listen to Hitler's.

The madman

Throughout the last months of 1937 the Gestapo detected hints of several plots that were plausible threats to the Third Reich. Some of these were generated by patriots in Czechoslovakia and Switzerland, others by dissident exiles who had made their way to London. Hitler had already reabsorbed the Saarland, restored the German military presence in the Rhineland and blatantly ignored the restrictions on German rearmament laid down at Versailles. Plotting by the Czechs was to be expected because Hitler was obviously planning to dismember their country, which had come into being as a result of the hated 1919 Peace Settlement.

Nazi agitation among the German-speaking element in the Sudeten borderlands was whipping up an unstoppable demand for union with the Third Reich. And occasional mutterings by senior Nazis about the need to increase German interest in Switzerland were enough to send shudders through Swiss patriots and spur them into thinking about action as well. London was beginning to look like a safer haven than Paris to the many dissidents who had escaped from Nazi Germany. Nazi agents operating in London were soon busy sending back reports of resistance plots and plans, circles of dissident agents and secret consignments of propaganda and arms. Yet little of this secret opposition activity came to much.

The man who came closest to killing Hitler in late 1937 was probably Josef Thomas, a working man from Elberfeld, a suburb of the busy industrial city of Wuppertal in Westphalia. Before the rise of the Nazis, Wuppertal was a hotbed of trade union militancy, with a tradition of support for socialist parties in the ballot box and a taste for stronger communist sentiments in the bars at night. Once Hitler was in power, many of Wuppertal's left-wing activists enjoyed periods of 'protective custody' at the Kemna camp in the district of Barmen on the eastern flank of the city. Kemna was one of the earliest camps built by the Nazis and it opened for business on 5 July 1933. It was not an extermination camp but a place where political opponents could be concentrated and re-educated. The Kemna curriculum included interrogation, torture, humiliation and continual beatings, while rotten fish smeared with vomit, excrement and engine oil was frequently on the menu. Many prisoners died at Kemna and numerous others were mentally disturbed and scarred for the rest of their lives.

The Nazis learned a lot from this first experience of running a concentration camp. They discovered that their brutal methods worked: the most fervent communist could be turned into a pliant automaton quickly and cheaply. They also ascertained that Kemna was too close to Wuppertal. Residents complained about the howls from tortured prisoners and the smell of latrines that drifted across from the camp and into their gardens. Future camps would need to be located further away from built-up areas.

Josef Thomas may well have been a graduate of Kemna. His actions certainly seemed to be those of a mentally deranged man out for revenge at all costs. He had a gun and the ammunition for it. He made no secret of the fact that he wanted to kill Hitler and Göring and that he was going to Berlin to get rid of both of them. On 26 November 1937 he walked into the Reich Chancellery, making no attempt to hide his weapon. He managed to walk around the corridors for a short spell, looking for his targets, until he was detained by the Gestapo. The Nazi authorities wasted little time in dealing with him. They judged that he was a mental patient and they knew exactly how to deal with that kind of ailment. Josef Thomas of Elberfeld quickly disappeared and was never heard of again.

CHAPTER 9

September 1938
Plotting for Peace

The number of men in the shock squad was secret and it remains unknown to this day. It would need to have been between 50 and 60 strong in order to be sure of carrying out its mission successfully. A supply of weapons and ammunition was already waiting for the squad in several safe houses and apartments, most of them close to key buildings in the governmental quarter of central Berlin. These caches of arms had been supplied from the arsenal of the Abwehr, or German military intelligence, and then deployed unobtrusively throughout the late summer as the central European crisis intensified.

The lead plotters had drawn up their plans carefully, checking the details by walking and driving around the centre of the city and carefully examining the entrances and exits to the buildings that would need to be closed down on the day. Senior officials in the police, the army and the security services who were thought to be sympathetic had been identified. Their willingness to support the plot, or at least refrain from interfering with it, had been assured. Detachments of Wehrmacht infantry commanded by officers who could be trusted would have several key functions to perform. Central Berlin would be quarantined and key government ministries that dealt with defence and security matters would be sealed off. Troops would take control of all radio stations and communications throughout the city and transport points would be monitored and closed if necessary. Critically, hostile SS personnel in and around Berlin would be neutralized.

As the city was being closed down, the telephones in the safe houses would ring to activate the shock squad. These self-selected men would carry out the bloody end of the business. They were a mixture of idealistic army officers, intelligence personnel and German nationalists of various denominations, all united in their distaste for Hitler and his Nazi gang. Their target was the Reich Chancellery. If necessary, they would fight their way in and make for the rooms that Hitler was known to use. Some of the plotters believed that once captured he would be taken for trial or simply locked away in a lunatic asylum. Others in the shock squad had been given secret orders to kill him on the spot.

Unlike many of the earlier attempts to murder Hitler, this was not the hopeful dream of a desperate loner or a small but ill-equipped cabal with little chance of getting close enough to strike out the man they despised. Instead, it was a well-resourced operation that had been carefully and thoroughly planned by men with a military and intelligence background. Knowledge of the plot, and tacit support for it, reached up into the highest levels of the German establishment. It was not a simple attempt at assassination but a *coup d'état* designed to destabilize and overthrow the entire Nazi regime. Arresting and eradicating Hitler was a necessary part of the exercise but not an end in itself. The plotters were motivated by the far more important aim of saving Germany from stumbling once again into a catastrophic, unwinnable European war on two fronts.

The Sudetenland problem

On 12 March 1938 Hitler entered his homeland as its leader. For 20 years he had dreamed of incorporating Austria within a Greater Germany. The motorcade procession from his boyhood home of Linz to the heart of Vienna, where he stayed at the Hotel Imperial, was met by huge, ecstatic crowds. Now his mind turned to his next territorial target. This was the land that had been part of Bohemia and Moravia in the days of the Austrian Empire and now formed the rim of western Czechoslovakia. Hitler detested Czechoslovakia. It was a mixed-race state created by the hated Paris Peace Settlement in 1919. The ethnic Germans within its borders, some 23 per cent of the population, were subject to rule by the Slav majority.

The idea of Germans being governed by *Untermenschen* disgusted Hitler. Some National Socialist racial theorists drew a distinction between the Czechs and the inferior Slavs further east. They argued that the Czechs had been exposed to German culture for many centuries and had been improved by that contact. As a result, they were capable of being Aryanized to some extent and could be useful in organizing and managing the lower forms of Slav in the vast German Empire that would soon stretch to the Urals. Hitler wasn't convinced. His energy was now directed towards the enslavement and destruction of his abominable neighbours. Two weeks after his Viennese triumph, Hitler met Konrad Henlein, the leader of the separatist Sudeten German Party and his stooge in Czechoslovakia. He encouraged Henlein to carry on agitating for greater autonomy for the Sudetenland and assured him of his personal support. By mid-September, Henlein's curiously well-resourced campaign of agitation and provocation would boil over into an undeclared civil war between Sudeten Nazi partisans and the Czech authorities.

A season of intimidation

Throughout the summer months of 1938, Hitler made a great show of displaying his malicious intentions towards Czechoslovakia, making numerous references to his discontent with the Sudeten situation in public speeches throughout Germany. His discussions with Polish and Hungarian diplomats about the mutual benefits of dismembering Czechoslovakia were hardly secret. In late May, large-scale Wehrmacht exercises close to the Czech border provoked a civilian panic in Prague and throughout August Hitler was very visibly planning for the coming war. He was photographed taking a keen interest in military manoeuvres at Grafenwöhr on the Czech frontier and talked about nothing else at a three-hour-long meeting with his senior commanders on 10 August. Five days later, he and his generals gathered at the huge Wehrmacht base at Jüterbog, south of Berlin, to watch an artillery bombardment demolishing a massive replica of a stretch of the Czech fortifications.

In case any foreign diplomats and correspondents failed to understand the significance of that event, the elaborate exercise was repeated two days later at the army training camp at Döberitz, just outside Berlin. On 18 August the visiting French Air Force chief of staff General Vuillemin received an aerial salute from the Luftwaffe. The carefully orchestrated and cleverly prolonged fly-past convinced Vuillemin that Germany had achieved overwhelming superiority in the air. His gloomy report of the event caused deep despair in French government circles. The Hungarian leader Admiral Horthy was then given the five-star treatment on his visit to Berlin. Hitler hoped that images of German–Hungarian solidarity would further demoralize the Czechs, who already feared a two-pronged attack in the event of military confrontation – however, Horthy responded rather cautiously to Hitler's plans and offers.

The cameraman standing on the lead car catches the march of the Mercs at the Rathausplatz, Vienna in April 1938. Hitler made sure his success in annexing Austria did not go unnoticed by the rest of the world.

The Westwall

In June 1938 Germany began to upgrade its defences along its western borders with the Netherlands, Belgium and France. And on 12 September Hitler made a speech to the army, emphasizing the extensive improvements that had already been made to the Westwall, the fortifications that would later be nicknamed the Siegfried Line by British troops. His real audience, however, was in Paris and London. Operation Green, his plan to invade Czechoslovakia, had always depended on French and British indecision. Hitler knew it was vital to isolate the Czechs by dispiriting their dithering Western allies. And in any case, a stronger Westwall would be needed if the French and British did come to the rescue of the Czechs. Hitler doubted that they would, but it was an important display of German resolve. The following day he told the world that the Sudeten Germans, victims of persistent Slav oppression, 'were not friendless and will not be deserted'.

Growing disquiet

Like Hitler, Friedrich Wilhelm Heinz was a patriotic soldier who was injured in the last months of the Great War and spent his time thereafter recuperating in hospital and raging against the Armistice sell-out. Heinz was badly injured again in 1919, fighting as a volunteer in the struggle to stop the German city of Posen from becoming Polish Poznan. And again like Hitler he got involved in the army's education organization in 1919, where he met many like-minded and bitter comrades, including Hermann Ehrhardt and the naval officer Wilhelm Canaris. After a spell in Ehrhardt's Freikorps, Heinz joined the terrorist Organization Consul and co-operated in the murder of several Weimar politicians, including the foreign minister Walther Rathenau. Although he was a member of the Viking League, he helped the Nazis build up their SA presence in the region of Hesse. Not entirely convinced by Hitler, Heinz joined *Der Stahlhelm* or Steel Helmet, an anti-Weimar organization of former soldiers that was the largest paramilitary group in Germany throughout the 1920s.

When Heinz briefly joined the NSDAP in 1929, he naturally gravitated towards its action men such as the Strasser brothers rather than Hitler who was, publicly at least, committed at that time to seeking power through the ballot box. Heinz's impatient revolutionary aspirations led to his speedy expulsion from the Nazi Party. When he tried to reapply in 1933 he was rejected. Angry with Hitler, he retired from politics in 1936 and returned to the ranks of the army, now reorganized as the Wehrmacht. There he met and was cultivated by his old friend Canaris, a rising star in the Abwehr military intelligence department in the Ministry of War. A natural rebel and discontent, in the summer of 1938 Heinz was hard at work helping to plan an attack that would stop the heart of the Nazi government by storming the Reich Chancellery. The honour of leading the shock squad that would find and liquidate Hitler was to be his.

Hans Oster was a career soldier who entered the Imperial army in 1907, distinguished himself on the Western Front and ended the war on the General Staff. Oster was one of the bright young men kept on after 1919, when most army officers were pensioned off to satisfy the Versailles restrictions on the future size of the German military. By late 1933 he was working in the Abwehr where, like Wilhelm Heinz, he came into contact with Canaris. As a conservative patriot, Oster had initially accepted Hitler's coming to power but as a Christian he watched the consolidation of Hitler's dictatorship with foreboding. The traditional influence and prestige of the army was gradually being overshadowed by the fanatical and cultish SS. He was increasingly appalled by the illegality and amorality of the policies and actions of the Nazi government. The SS targets in the 1934 purge had included a number of senior army and Abwehr officers, who were murdered in cold blood without trial for simply failing to toe the party line. Oster witnessed the growing persecution of Jews in the streets of the Third Reich and, as with many other Christian Germans, the mad frenzy of Kristallnacht was a defining moment in his life. He would eventually be dismissed from the Abwehr in 1943 when the Gestapo discovered that he had sheltered Jews.

Like many honourable army officers, Oster was also vexed and outraged by the public humiliation of two senior and much-esteemed army commanders in 1938. General Werner von Blomberg fell from grace when it was alleged that his new wife was a convicted prostitute and a purveyor of pornography, but Blomberg stood by her and refused Hitler's advice that he annul the marriage. The scandal was used by Hitler and Göring to engineer Blomberg's resignation. False charges of homosexual behaviour were then brought against General von Fritsch. According to a 'reliable witness' called Schmidt, Fritsch had been seen participating in a sexual act in a public lavatory with a well-known male prostitute, who went by the name of Bavarian Joe. The charges were outrageous, but Goebbels nevertheless ensured that the salacious details were given full coverage in the press. Fritsch was eventually acquitted but he had been deeply humiliated and never regained the heights of senior command. Several

Like so many German officers, Hans Oster at first welcomed the Nazi regime, but his mind changed in 1934 after the Night of the Long Knives and other atrocities perpetrated by Hitler and his followers.

high-ranking colleagues who had supported Fritsch throughout the farrago demonstrated their anger by resigning and the standing of the army in the public imagination was diminished. As had been planned from the beginning, Hitler used these scandals to weaken the Army High Command. More pliable men were promoted to a new Supreme Command of the Armed Forces, or OKW. The 'reliable' Herr Schmidt, a professional blackmailer of homosexual men, was conveniently found dead soon afterwards in murky circumstances.

Throughout the 1930s many individual Germans in positions of authority felt a deep and growing disquiet about the direction of the Third Reich, but until 1938 most of them tended to keep their private thoughts to themselves. Hitler was not only powerful but popular. He had righted some of the wrongs of Versailles and he had restored German national pride. As conservative patriots, Hitler's doubters and critics were prepared to push their concerns to one side for the national good. The Czech crisis in summer 1938 changed everything. Hitler was now taking an immense diplomatic risk of a different degree. As he strode towards confrontation, a very loose network of informed men in positions of authority began to coalesce. The tension of those months created an atmosphere of speculation in which it was easier to express fears and concerns to others, and to identify fellow-minded colleagues.

Plot to stop the Austrian corporal

A plot materialized. There were many in offices throughout Berlin who knew something about it. Some played an active part and others, just as importantly, stood back and said and did nothing. For many of these men, the Czech crisis plot was their first experience of resistance to Hitler. Most of them had come to a decision to oppose Hitler and the Nazi regime by the same path as Heinz and Oster. They shared a deep sense of repugnance at the illegality of many of the regime's actions and were shocked by the fundamental inhumanity of its world-view. Those in the 'network' who were military men were also alarmed by Hitler's territorial ambitions, which would almost certainly lead Germany into a war, first with the Western democracies and then with the Slavic powers in the East. These were men who had long pondered and analysed the strategic reasons for the failure of 1918. They were convinced that despite its outstanding military traditions and its current short-term industrial superiority, Germany could not win a long war fought on two fronts. The Wehrmacht could perform mighty heroics in the field but the Royal Navy's blockade of the seas, combined with potential Soviet numbers on land and in the air, would always

Old-school German officers such as (from the left) General Werner von Fritsch, General Werner von Blomberg and Admiral Raeder often became prey for the Nazis.

give Germany's enemies the advantage in a longer conflict. General Beck said as much to Hitler's face before resigning from the General Staff in August 1938. Beck and generals Halder and Witzleben all knew about the plot in Berlin and supported it in varying degrees.

The aristocratic lawyer Ewald von Kleist-Schmenzin made little effort to disguise his dislike of Hitler and he pointedly refused to fly the swastika over his castle. He held no office in the Third Reich, but as the Czech crisis deepened he was well placed to travel to Great Britain as a private citizen. In London he tried to alert the British to the extent of the opposition to Hitler that existed in Berlin and he urged his influential British friends to convince Chamberlain to stand by the Czechs at all costs and call Hitler's bluff. Hjalmar Schacht, Hitler's economist, made the very same points to his many contacts in London, Paris and Amsterdam. Many of these men wanted Hitler brought to trial to answer for the crimes committed by his government since 1933, but putting Hitler in the dock hadn't exactly worked in 1923. Oster preferred to have Hitler declared insane. The jurist Hans von Dohnányi agreed and made his contribution to the plot by inviting his father-in-law, the psychiatrist Professor Karl Bonhöffer, to suggest eminent colleagues who could form a suitable panel for despatching Hitler to his padded cell.

Behind all of these men was Canaris. His career began at the age of 17 in the German Imperial Navy and in the First World War he served with Germany's ill-fated blue water fleet in the Pacific and the South Atlantic. He was one of the few crewmen to make it back to the Fatherland. Later in his career he served as a U-boat commander in the Mediterranean. An exceptionally able man, he spoke six languages well and he was also very wealthy and well connected. In post-war Germany, he shared many views with the Austrian corporal, believing that the Jews and the communists needed to be rooted out. That was difficult work and if Hitler's gang had to commit the odd brutality to clean out the stables, then so be it. Canaris also hated the Treaty of Versailles and recognized Hitler as a man who would rebuild the German fleet that had been scuttled in the cold waters of Scapa Flow in 1919. Canaris became head of the Abwehr in 1935 and when he met with Hitler both men enjoyed their discussions and their meeting of minds. They had much in common at that point in time: Canaris may have first given Hitler the idea of forcing Jews to wear a Star of David badge to better identify the enemy within.

Three years later, Germany's military spymaster had definitely begun to moderate his affection for the Führer and his works. Like many conservatives, in Canaris's view Hitler was only meant to be a necessary but temporary means to an end. Hitler's early diplomatic triumphs – returning the Saarland to the Reich and putting soldiers back into the Rhineland – were effectively domestic matters, popular within Germany and easily explained away to the French and the British as an understandable reaction to the over-harsh Treaty of 1919. The annexation of Austria in March 1938 was a similar tidying up of the map and, after all, hadn't the Austrians endorsed the union with Germany in massive numbers when they voted in the plebiscite? But confronting the feisty, well-defended Czechs, who had the French and British empires on their side, was a much riskier proposal. As other military theorists of his age had deduced, it seemed that the Austrian adventurer had taken Germany far enough but had now outlived his usefulness.

Ready for war

Hitler was certainly taking a big risk by going to war with the Czechs. They had read *Mein Kampf*, they had listened to Hitler's radio rants on the theme of *Lebensraum* and his plans to subjugate the lesser peoples of eastern Europe and they were prepared for a bloody ethnic war to the death. They knew they had no choice and they certainly didn't trust the French and the British to come to their aid, but they could at least choose the field of battle. Much of the disputed borderland was heavily forested, hilly and in places mountainous, so it could be made to favour the defender. During the 1930s, the Czechs built more than 260 large, heavy concrete blast-proof blockhouses for their troops at key points along the frontier and over 10,000 pillboxes for heavy machine-gunners were positioned at bridges, road junctions and along the railway lines. The army manning these defences was very well trained and the troops knew they were fighting for the very existence of their people. And it was a well-supplied and well-equipped army, thanks to the massive and innovative Škoda works at Plzeň in western Bohemia.

In the first half of the 20th century, Škoda was one of the largest arms manufacturers in the world. It was also one of the best. In the later 1930s German military analysts who examined Škoda products were impressed by their quality and efficiency, but they were dismayed when they examined Škoda's new LT35 battle tank. It was the finest weapon of its kind anywhere in the world at that point in time. Between 1939 and 1942 it would go on to parade through the conquered cities of Poland and France and to wreak havoc in much of western Russia. By then it bore the insignia of the Wehrmacht and

Admiral Canaris was the head of German counter-espionage, which gave him unique insight into the plans of the Nazi regime and those plotting against it.

was known as the Panzer 35t. With strong fortifications, excellent weaponry and a people fighting for its very existence, Czechoslovakia was a much stronger foe than Nazi propagandists liked to suggest. Even Hitler was beginning to rethink his strategy as the outbreak of war seemed ever closer.

A weekend in Prague?

Hitler had boasted of being in Prague within two or three days of the outbreak of war, but now he was privately admitting that cracking the Czechs would be a very tough proposition. The campaign might well drag on, given the undoubted strength of their fortified positions. In the first days of September, he was burning much midnight oil with his senior officers, peering at the plans and maps for Operation Green and looking for a route to a speedy victory. His intimates had not seen him so nervous since he defied the League of Nations and sent troops into the Rhineland in 1935. All of this was as predicted or hoped for by the plotters back in Berlin. Tough Czech resistance and mounting German casualties would throw a new critical light on the Führer's abilities as a commander and his feet of clay would be exposed. Nevertheless, in towns and villages throughout the Sudetenland, Konrad Henlein and his 'civilian' paramilitaries were ready and waiting for the signal to spark off some bloody atrocity that would kick-start another European war. And in their safe houses in Berlin, Wilhelm Heinz and his shock squad were also already in position, on alert and waiting for their call.

British intervention

Enter Neville Chamberlain. On 14 September the British Embassy in Berlin handed Herr Hitler a note indicating that the British prime minister was willing to fly to Germany to try and find a peaceful solution to the Czech crisis. The world's attention was diverted away from the armed tensions along the Czech border towards the diplomatic drama that would be played out over the next 16 days at Berchtesgaden, Bad Godesberg and finally at the four-power Munich Conference.

Henlein and his men were told by Berlin to be patient, but the Czechs quickly beefed up their forces in front positions and easily wiped up the small localized attempts to foment a pro-German uprising. Having lost the initiative, Henlein and his key supporters fled over the German border, but on 30 September Chamberlain and the French agreed to a document that effectively ordered the Czechs to evacuate the Sudetenland. The withdrawal of their forces was to begin the following day. Through his sheer swagger, Hitler had won everything he wanted without risking a single German life.

The price of appeasement

With their Sudetenland defences lost, the fate of the Czechs was sealed. Hitler could dismember the rest of Czechoslovakia whenever it was convenient. Throughout the Third Reich, there was a further unassailable wave of affection for the Great Leader. Hitler had never been so popular with his people and he had never seemed so invincible. The Berlin plotters had needed to catch the German public in a downbeat, pensive mood, but as a result of Chamberlain's dramatic intervention, Hitler was untouchable. To kill him now would only spawn a second Stab-in-the-Back legend even greater than the 1918 first edition. The shock squad was stood down and their arms were secretly conveyed back to the Abwehr stores. On 2 October, Hitler and Goebbels met to discuss their future tactics and set a timescale for dealing with the remnants of the Czechoslovakian Republic. The following day the new ruler of the Sudetenland toured his latest possession as his legions marched ahead to set up the new German administration. He stopped at the border town of Eger and gave a speech in its pretty main square. For the first time, Hitler used the expression *Grossdeutsches Reich* or Greater German Empire. On 6 October Hitler and Goebbels went walking in the Sudeten woods, stopping to look with interest at the impressive line of Czech fortifications. Hitler murmured: 'We would have lost a lot of blood here, you know ...'

CHAPTER 10

November 1938
The Christian Assassin

By 1938, many aspects of public life in Germany had been Nazified. The traditional high points in the annual calendar, marking the seasons and the Christian festivals, had been augmented by new National Socialist celebrations inspired by key events in the life of the Führer and the history of the Party: his birthday on 20 April, his assumption of power on 30 January, the Nuremberg Party Rally on the autumnal equinox and the commemoration of the Munich Putsch on 8 and 9 November. The Führer's attendance at these and other significant occasions was inescapable and the highly choreographed and ritualistic nature of these major Nazi gatherings meant that Hitler's movements on those particular days, plus the times of his arrival and departure, could almost be predicted. These were the points in the year when the Reich's security organizations had to be at their most alert.

Totalitarian security

By 1938, they had become experienced at protecting their leader at the many different kinds of public appearance that he was required to make in the course of his duties. Five years of Nazi clampdown throughout German society had, of course, wiped out many of the sources of potential danger from oppositionists. Thousands of potential troublemakers with anti-Nazi sympathies had found their way to the re-education camps, or worse. The state's security apparatus had also established systems of information-gathering that stretched all the way down to the local *Blockleiters*. These were the watchful Party Wardens or 'snoops' found in every residential building or neighbourhood, who monitored the activities and attitudes of their neighbours, recording details of those who showed insufficient enthusiasm for life in the New Germany. By 1938, the men in charge of Hitler's safety could reassure themselves that the Great Leader was fairly safe from public attack by a native German assassin. It was, however, impossible for them to plan against the kind of assassin who stalked the Führer in the later months of that year; an unknown foreign assassin with no political background, who travelled to Germany solely because he believed it was his divine duty to kill the Austrian Antichrist.

The Swiss crusader

Maurice Bavaud was a French-speaking Swiss citizen born in 1916 into a large Catholic family in the western town of Neuchâtel. The family was pious, conventional and petit bourgeois: Maurice's father worked for the Swiss postal service while his mother ran a small grocery corner-shop. Those who remembered the young Bavaud described a calm, pleasant, well-mannered youth. His education was unexceptional and when he left school in 1932 he initially planned to train as a draughtsman. But like many confused young men coming to maturity in the wake of the Great Depression, he was aware of the economic and political turmoil across Europe. He read socialist and communist pamphlets and toyed with the idea of joining the Swiss fascist party, the Front National. By 1934, however, possibly as a result of his Christian upbringing and the direction of his devout father, he was considering training as a Catholic missionary to the French colonies in Africa. He enrolled the following spring at a seminary in Saint-Brieuc, on the northern coast of Brittany. There he was known to be thoughtful and fond of reading philosophy. He recited Swiss songs and poems to his fellow students and contributed to the Gregorian chant in the chapel. At Saint-Brieuc he also met an unusual but compelling fellow seminarian called Marcel Gerbohay, who came from a village near Rennes.

Mystic resistance

Gerbohay exerted a powerful political influence over Maurice and invited him to join a small secret society called La Compagnie du Mystère, which was dedicated to the destruction of communism and the restoration of the Romanov dynasty to the throne of Russia. Gerbohay confided to Bavaud that he was a surviving member of the Romanov family and the trusting student priest seems to have believed him. Through Gerbohay, Bavaud was introduced to the ideas of the various mystical ultra-Catholic organizations throughout Europe that

Maurice Bavaud was a placid Swiss theology student who came to believe it was his Christian duty to assassinate Hitler.

were sworn to fighting the new secular ideologies of communism and National Socialism. It was thanks to these political discussions with this strange friend that the placid Swiss theology student decided that it was his Christian duty to assassinate Adolf Hitler.

By the summer of 1938, Bavaud had come to believe that the German leader had abandoned his earlier anti-Bolshevik rhetoric and was planning a future of coexistence between Nazi Germany and the Soviet Union. Many Catholics in Germany and throughout Europe had become increasingly apprehensive about the atheistic tone that underpinned much of Nazi ideology and culture. Five years into the Reich, there had been enough instances of enthusiastic Nazi leaders seeking to humiliate those who upheld traditional Christian values and beliefs. The growing use of neopagan symbolism in Nazi ritual and propaganda offered further proof that Hitler was a threat to the continuing existence of the Roman Catholic Church in Germany. In addition, Hitler was clearly set upon absorbing all of the German-speaking territories in central Europe within his Thousand Year Reich, a policy that threatened the unity and very existence of Bavaud's Swiss homeland. In June he left the seminary for good, returning home to spend the summer improving his knowledge of German and planning a way of destroying the man he now believed was a threat to all humanity and an agent of Satan.

A useful kinsman

Early on the morning of 9 October 1938, Maurice left a farewell note for his family and took the train to the lovely spa town of Baden-Baden in the Black Forest. Later that day he introduced himself to his bemused and very distant relatives who lived there. They went by the name of Gutterer and were related to Maurice through a sister of his grandmother. It's likely that they had never before set eyes on the quiet Swiss lad with imperfect German who stood at their door, but Bavaud had a very good reason for making the Gutterer home his first port of call in Hitler's Reich. The senior member of the household, Leopold, had already done well under the Nazi regime and was destined for even higher things. Leopold had joined the NSDAP in 1925 when the fortunes of the Party were at a low ebb.

Hitler had spent most of the previous year in Landsberg Prison and in his absence the Party had stalled, losing more than half of its seats in the Reichstag elections in December 1924. This was partly because the strained economic and political situation in Germany was now improving, thanks to American loans and a better spirit of international co-operation between the democratic government in Weimar and Germany's former enemies. The bitterness of the immediate post-war years was evaporating, as were the hopes of the extreme populist parties on the left and right. By joining the Party when he did, Leopold Gutterer therefore gave proof that he was a true believer, rather than one of the multitude of fellow-travellers who would only discover their National Socialist convictions at a much later, more convenient point in time.

The fruits of loyalty

An effective and hard-working journalist and editor, by 1930 Leopold was an important Nazi publicist and publisher. After 1933 he was well rewarded for his loyalty and efforts, quickly becoming a senior official in Joseph Goebbels' Ministry of Public Enlightenment and Propaganda, where he was responsible for organizing the main public displays of Nazi pomp such as the key Party rallies in Berlin and Nuremberg. As State Secretary in 1941 he introduced the legislation forcing German Jews to wear the yellow *Judenstern*, as their Polish co-religionists had done since 1939. Highly regarded in the top echelons of the Party, he was invited to the secret Wannsee conference in January 1942, which was convened by Reinhard Heydrich to co-ordinate the efficient implementation of the Final Solution to the Jewish Question.

As early as 1938, Maurice Bavaud knew that his distant in-law already enjoyed frequent personal contact with Goebbels and other important Party officials. It was even possible that at some point Leopold might be in close proximity to the Führer himself. This was the idea that had lured Bavaud to Baden-Baden. By appearing to be a fervent National Socialist he hoped to ingratiate himself with Leopold and perhaps enjoy a degree of useful patronage. He might then be able to engineer an opportunity to get closer to his ultimate target.

His potential mentor and patron was no fool, however, and he viewed the sudden appearance of this little-known relative with suspicion. He made it clear that Maurice could hope for no support from him, nor should he expect a helpful letter of introduction and commendation. In fact, Leopold seems to have been so wary of his young Swiss visitor that he alerted the Gestapo to his presence in the area. With no promise of help from his Gutterer kin, limited funds and little prospect of finding work, given his limited German, Maurice decided to get closer to the Antichrist as quickly as possible and under his own steam. He set out on a desperate journey that in three weeks would take him across Germany to all three of Hitler's main bases: Berlin, Munich and the Berghof. At one of these, he hoped to get within a gunshot of his great foe.

A view to the kill

On 21 October Bavaud arrived in Berlin, having covered his tracks by telling the Gutterers that he was heading to the busy industrial town of Mannheim, 70 miles (113 km) away, to look for work. He was now armed with a Schmeisser 6.35 mm (0.25 in) handgun, which was powerful enough to kill at close range and could be easily concealed in a coat pocket. All that was missing was his target, for Hitler was not in the capital but at his Alpine complex, the Berghof near Obersalzberg, in deepest Bavaria. Four days later, Bavaud stepped off the train at Berchtesgaden, in the valley beneath Hitler's mountain retreat, only to find that his prey had eluded him again, for the Führer had moved on to Munich.

This time, rather than chasing after the fox Bavaud spent several days walking alone in the hills around Obersalzberg, examining the lie of the land, monitoring the security arrangements at the Berghof and learning how to use his gun by shooting at trees in the forests. In Berchtesgaden, he fell into conversation with Karl Deckert, a captain in the local police who had some understanding of the Führer's security arrangements. Deckert assumed that Bavaud's desire to meet Hitler in person stemmed from the usual adulation that Hitler had inspired in so many ardent young men across interwar Europe. He advised Maurice that the chances of meeting Hitler without a letter of recommendation from a foreign embassy or a senior political figure were nil. However, if he simply wished to see the Führer, Deckert suggested that Maurice watch the annual parade through Munich on 9 November, when Hitler and his closest cronies marched through the city to remember their comrades who had fallen in the disastrous putsch in 1923.

Hunting down Hitler

Bavaud took up the captain's suggestion and found a room in Munich on 31 October, where he spent the next week planning his course of action. He repeatedly walked the route of the procession, thinking of possible vantage points that would get him within 25 or so feet (7.6 m) of Hitler, the effective range of his weapon. At first, he planned simply to run out from the crowd towards Hitler and shoot him down in the street but he quickly dismissed this idea, probably when he saw the SA and the Hitler Youth rehearsing for the big event. Two ranks of Brownshirts would be lining the entire route, which began at the Bürgerbräukeller on the eastern bank of the Isar river and then passed through the medieval old town to stately Königsplatz, where the 16 men who had died in the putsch were interred in two vast Honour Temples. Fortunately, Bavaud managed to blag a complimentary ticket for one of the temporary grandstands, by posing as a reporter for a Swiss newspaper. His seat was at a point near the Church of the Holy Spirit, where the route narrowed and turned. Here there was a good chance that on the day those in the procession would have to slow down to make their way through an old stone archway. Even better, his ticket was for a seat in one of the rows closest to the street.

Just a shot away

This was only the fifth year that the Nazi Party leadership had amassed in Munich to pay their respects to their dead – the ceremony had been cancelled in 1934, as there were lingering doubts about the loyalty of the SA Brownshirts after their leadership had been massacred in the Night of the Long Knives that June. Each year the ritual had grown more impressive. After briefly addressing the longest-serving Party faithful at the Bürgerbräukeller, Hitler set out to retrace the steps he had taken in his first aborted attempt at achieving power, 15 years before. Only one man preceded him and that was Jakob Grimminger, a Party member since 1922 and wearer of the Blood Order Medal, a decoration restricted to those Party members who had taken part in the attempted coup. Grimminger was the honorary standard-bearer of the most sacred of all Nazi artefacts, the *Blutfahne* or Flag of Blood, said to have been dipped in the flowing blood of all 16 Nazi martyrs that day.

Hitler followed immediately behind the banner in the midst of a phalanx of Party leaders and the *Alte Kämpfer*, the old fighters who bore decorations such as the Coburg Badge, to show they had fought alongside Hitler in the earlier and bloodiest street battles against the German Communist Party. Then came the massed ranks of SS, SA and Hitler Youth units from throughout the Reich. Bavaud would have known that Hitler was approaching long before he saw him. The constant drumming, the blare of the marching bands, the crunch of 10,000 boots on street cobbles and the rising tension among the waiting crowd all signalled that the great man was near. Then a hushed expectation settled across the grandstand as the tip of the bloodstained flag suddenly emerged through the covered archway and the crowd caught its first glimpse of the brown-shirted Führer. At that point, Bavaud released his tight grip upon the pistol in the pocket of his heavy overcoat and sat back in despair.

There were three unexpected obstacles to getting a clear shot away, even though the target right in front of him was walking at a slow, sombre pace. His view of Hitler was partially obscured by the wavering arms of those around him, all extended in the Sieg Heil salute. The other Party leaders abreast of Hitler, including the corpulent Göring and the broad-backed Julius Streicher, were walking in loose, irregular file and so interfering with Bavaud's sight line. And to his dismay, Hitler was not walking in the centre of the Nazi column as he had expected but was stationed on the far side of the street, almost 50 feet (15 m) away from the grandstand and well out of the Schmeisser's killing range. Within a few short steps, Hitler had moved further on and was shielded by the heads and flags of those coming behind him. Bavaud's best chance of slaying the Antichrist had vanished.

Forgery and failure

As Bavaud considered his next move, he remembered Captain Deckert's advice about letters of introduction. Over the next two days he forged two plausible letters, the first handwritten and purporting to be from the former French prime minister Pierre Flandin. The second typed letter was 'from' Pierre Taittinger, the champagne magnate and a prominent supporter of right-wing political groups in interwar France. On consecutive days Maurice used one letter to try and gain access to the Berghof compound and the other to try to enter the Brown House, headquarters of the NSDAP in Munich. In both cases, Bavaud claimed that he was carrying an additional highly confidential letter for the Führer's eyes only. This desperate ruse got him no further than the first level of security.

Bavaud spent a few more days wandering around Berchtesgaden, failing to see any way that he could get close to Hitler. Then he made two more journeys across Bavaria by train to intercept him, only to find that the Führer had been hurtling in the exact opposite direction. Bavaud now ran out of money and hope, so he abandoned his mission and stowed aboard a train bound for France. At Augsburg, a wary ticket inspector handed the suspicious foreigner over to the Gestapo. Initially, his misdemeanours seemed relatively minor: travelling without a ticket and being in possession of a gun without having the necessary papers on his person. However, the discovery of his abandoned luggage in his Berlin lodgings made the Gestapo much more curious. His bag contained maps of central Munich and the Obersalzberg area, plus a cache of ammunition.

The House of Death

After many months of intensive interrogation, Bavaud stood trial at the People's Court in Berlin on 18 December 1939. Found guilty of the attempted murder of 'a member of the Reich's government', he was sentenced to death by beheading and sent to the notorious House of Death at Plötzensee Prison in the northern suburbs of Berlin. He then endured an agonizing wait of nearly 16 months before the punishment was carried out. His strange naivety, his lack of proper planning or adequate resources, his almost farcical failure to 'connect' with his target or to determine Hitler's whereabouts before meandering around the Reich and, above all, his puzzling defence that he was carrying out a spiritual mission: all of this flummoxed the Reich security organizations, who were accustomed to dealing with more rational and intelligible political prisoners. Finally, at dawn on 14 May 1941, Maurice Bavaud was put out of his misery. He was not awakened by the usual kitchen boy who doled out the breakfasts of cold, weak coffee and stale bread, but by the squad of officers and staff delegated to carry out his sentence. In the preparation room, his head and neck were shaved and his hands were tied behind his back. When he reached the execution room the long black curtain was lifted from the guillotine. Like many prisoners at Plötzensee, his last few seconds were spent strapped to a wooden board awaiting the touch of the heavy blade.

Classmates to the end

Under intense 'interrogation' by the Gestapo, Bavaud had been forced to offer his tormentors some names: those of friends and family and anyone who had ever spoken about politics with him. He had eventually mentioned his fellow seminarian, Marcel Gerbohay. Gerbohay's name also appeared in some of Bavaud's letters to his family back in Neuchâtel. With his apparent links to secret Catholic political organizations and his pretensions to royal blood, Gerbohay was a character who clearly interested Bavaud's bored inquisitors. In the calamitous and chaotic spring of 1940, Gerbohay seems to have escaped to the relative safety of Vichy France. He was, however, betrayed by collaborators, who recognized him when he returned to his home village of Pacé in the Occupied Zone to see his ailing mother. Clearly the dangerous mastermind behind Bavaud's mission to Germany, Marcel Gerbohay was guillotined on 9 April 1943 in the same House of Death where his friend Maurice had perished.

CHAPTER 11

20 April 1939

A Room with a View

rather stiff and disciplined man with a thin military moustache was standing at the window of his apartment, looking out over the scene below. He was tall and quite slim for his age, which seemed to be about 50. Although he was not particularly handsome, his craggy, lived-in face and the smile that occasionally stretched across his slightly crooked mouth broadcast the fact that he was an alert, intelligent man, keenly interested in and engaged with the world around him. With some visible difficulty, he maintained the ramrod back of a man who knows how to endure long hours standing to attention on parade. The sharp observer might have noticed the man frequently feeling for and counting his fingers, as if to check that they were all still there. When he made a slight move nearer to the glass to get a better view of the street, he shuffled with his toes facing inwards as if it was painful for him to lift his legs properly. And as he leaned towards the window pane so he could focus his gaze on the men outside unloading timber and tools from a small convoy of trucks, his head fell a little too far forward, as if all the weighty matters within it were too much for his weakened neck. These infirmities and mannerisms were the result of serious injuries, the first of them sustained in his youth on the polo field when he had been crushed beneath his mount. A man who loved fast cars, he had inflicted further damage to his spine and neck in a bad car crash in Hungary in 1933, leaving him with a permanent stoop.

A soldier and a spy

On top of these impairments, he had all the usual scars of a professional career soldier who had served throughout the Great War in France and the Middle

East. He had seen his share of bloody conflict, particularly on the disastrous expedition to relieve Kut in Mesopotamia in 1916. Now, in the spring of 1939, he was living in a pleasant apartment just off the central government district of Berlin. It was a wealthy and attractive quarter and many of the local residents were employed in the nearby ministries or were representatives of international companies or foreign governments. All in all, the smart area and his airy apartment suited Colonel Noel Mason-Macfarlane DSO MC and Two Bars Croix de Guerre, the current British military attaché in Berlin who was based at the British Embassy, which was then still housed in the shabby Palais Strousberg on Wilhelmstrasse.

Mason-Mac, as he was known to his embassy colleagues, was a relatively new boy to Berlin. His advanced military education began within the Indian army at Staff College, Quetta, followed by regimental duties and a spell at the finishing school that was the Imperial Defence College at Buckingham Gate in London. He was then posted as a military attaché to Vienna, Budapest and Bern, where he reported to M3, the intelligence section at the War Office that monitored central Europe. Berlin was the logical next step in his upward career. Although he had only arrived in Berlin in January 1938, he well understood the reason for the noise and bustle beneath his window. Everywhere there were teams of workers, who were beginning to transform Berlin in preparation for what was planned to be the greatest celebration in the history of the city, the marking of the Führer's 50th birthday on 20 April. And in his well-situated apartment, Mason-Mac was working out how he could best help the party go off with a bang.

Happy birthday, mein Führer

From the outset, 20 April 1939 was designed to be a monumental national event that eclipsed even the impressive annual NSDAP parades in Nuremberg and Munich. It would demonstrate the unity of the entire German nation and the rediscovered military strength of its armed forces. Newspapers and radio continually reminded the German citizenry that this was their opportunity to thank the Führer for all the economic and political blessings that he had won for his people. Before Hitler there was only social chaos, economic blight, communist treachery, Jewish conspiracy, international humiliation and drastic territorial amputation, with millions of Germans doomed to live as slaves under foreign domination. But in a mere six years of unceasing labour, Hitler's Germany had not only become the wealthiest nation in Europe but it was also

Colonel Noel Mason-Macfarlane, DSO MC and Two Bars Croix de Guerre, was a brilliant shot and might have prevented World War II if those above him had only listened to his plan to eliminate Adolf Hitler.

the most respected and most feared. Its internal enemies had been suppressed, its economy had been rejuvenated by massive infrastructure and military spending, the insults of Versailles had been repudiated and almost all German speakers in Europe had been reincorporated within the enlarged Third Reich that now dominated the map of Europe. There was much to thank Hitler for in April 1939.

A German jamboree

Preparations for the big day had been going on since the first warm days of spring. The Prussian Siegessäule or victory column had been transplanted from its original position near the Reichstag to a pivotal location on the newly broadened East–West Axis highway that bisected western Berlin. In Albert Speer's megalomanic plans for a future capital city called Germania, this avenue would be rebranded as Triumphstrasse. For Hitler's birthday party the entire boulevard was being draped in countless vast swastika flags and dozens of searchlights were being installed around Berlin for the midnight lightning shows that the Nazi hierarchy enjoyed so much. The programme included smaller events confirming the superiority of German art, music and technology and in every public space in Berlin, whether concert hall, theatre or open-air *Platz*, a myriad of organizations would contribute to a jamboree of German-ness. Participants from official bodies in every part of the Reich would soon be swelling the numbers crowding into the capital. The big day would culminate in a colossal, swaggering exhibition of Nazi bombast, the military parade. This would include personnel from every branch of the German armed forces, accompanied by their technical and mechanized equipment, while massed formations of the Luftwaffe would circle continuously above.

Hitler did not just wish to remind his German subjects of the proud fruits of his labour. He was out to terrify his future victims, particularly his next target – the Poles. The parade was expected to take four hours to pass the temporary grandstands that contained German bigwigs and a horde of foreign dignitaries, but in the event it would take almost five. As a professional soldier and a military attaché, Mason-Macfarlane had spent a lifetime watching martial pomp, so he could be excused if he felt a little blasé about the forthcoming revelry. He had seen marching Germans before. But he was now pondering something very interesting about the preparations outside his apartment. He realized that the men in the street were about to build the podium from which Hitler would review his legions and it suddenly struck him just how close it was to his flat.

The plan to pick off Hitler

On the big day Hitler would be trapped on that podium for at least four hours: standing relatively still and maintaining an imperial posture throughout the parade, endlessly raising his right arm to acknowledge the homage of the men marching past below. Mason-Macfarlane estimated that the distance from his apartment to the podium was approximately 100 m (328 ft). It was almost certainly more than this, though. He probably used this low estimate to help persuade his superiors that his plan to assassinate Hitler in broad daylight, in the middle of Berlin and at the most public moment in the dictator's life, was perfectly feasible. The distance was certainly close enough for a competent marksman with a steady hand and a high-velocity rifle with a telescopic sight to do a clean job. Even better, Mason-Mac realized that if the sniper kept well back from the window and stood on a small landing in the flat, he could still see the target and the muzzle flash would not be spotted by the crowd below. This would make it more difficult for observers to work out where the bullet had come from. The ecstatic cheering of devoted Nazis, the blare of the brass bands, the rumbling of tanks on the ground and the droning of the aircraft above would more than mask the sound of the shot. And with an almost static target, an experienced killer would have all the time needed to pick his moment.

An obstinate Scot

Mason-Mac was determined to do the job himself. It was his plan. He had learned to shoot as a small boy on the family farm in Forfarshire and he had enjoyed a reputation as a good shot throughout his career in the army. He told a close friend and colleague that the job was 'as easy as winking and what's more, I'm thinking of doing it'. But he well understood the risks he was taking. The sniper who killed Hitler would instantly become the most hunted man in history. Even if he managed by some miracle to leave central Berlin undetected and then slip out of the Reich, he would never be safe. He would always be the Gestapo's first suspect, not just because he had lived close to the parade route but because he had made his distaste for the National Socialists quite public while mingling in Berlin's diplomatic circles. That meant he would be a marked man for the rest of his life, never safe from an avenging Nazi knife or bullet. The chances were he'd be dead within the week. On the other hand, he'd get a great deal of personal satisfaction from giving Herr Hitler a taste of his own medicine.

The Arch Thug

At the height of the *Anschluss* crisis in early 1938, Mason-Mac had driven into Austria to witness that historic country being gobbled up into the Nazi Empire of Greater Germany. En route to Vienna he had stopped at a garage near Hitler's birthplace of Linz just as a convoy of black Mercedes saloons hurtled by, bearing the Führer towards his triumphal entry into Vienna. He noted the sinister SS bodyguards 'bristling with tommy-guns' as they guarded the man he dubbed 'the Arch Thug'. In Mason-Mac's eyes, Hitler was little more than a cheap but clever gangster who had taken advantage of the despair that millions of Germans felt after more than a decade of depression and austerity. He had seized the moment to distort history, identify scapegoats and peddle a poisonous mixture of racism, populism and expansionism. Mason-Mac had witnessed the treatment of the Jews on Kristallnacht and had been disgusted by it. That September, he had been on the Czechoslovakian border and had seen the undeclared war fought by the Nazi Sudeten Freikorps against the legitimate Czech authorities. And he had gathered ample evidence of the enormous concentration of arms and men that were being stockpiled along the German–Polish border throughout the summer of 1939. It was clear to Mason-Mac that Hitler, having digested the remains of Czechoslovakia in the spring, was getting ready to launch an all-out war in the East.

This war would come quickly, Mason-Mac argued, because Germany had a significant advantage over both Poland and the Soviet Union in terms of war materiel and national readiness. But as Hitler also knew, the advantage was only temporary. The Führer was well aware that Germany's best chance of victory against Poland lay in a sudden attack in autumn before winter set in. In Mason-Mac's opinion this inevitable war could be averted with one bullet. He was well aware that while the charismatic Hitler had won over the masses, Germany's military elite had mixed feelings about their ultimate commander. If Hitler were to be taken out, Mason-Mac believed that the German High Command would intervene and stabilize the situation. There had been many signals to suggest that he was right. Later writers would often explain the rift between Hitler and his generals in terms of class snobbery: the aristocratic German generals looking down upon the ignorant Austrian corporal. In fact, the Wehrmacht's highly trained elite officers had analysed Hitler's future-view in great detail and many of them suspected they were being dragged into another unwinnable two-front war. They had no appetite for a repeat of 1914–18.

Kicked upstairs

Mason-Macfarlane shared his assassination plan with his superior, the British Ambassador in Berlin Sir Nevile Henderson, even though he knew he would get no support from that quarter. The two men did not get on. In many ways, Mason-Macfarlane, a man with a first-class brain and exceptional linguistic ability, was an outsider within the British establishment. Despite having attended Eton, he had never fully absorbed the imperial group-think that dominated the upper echelons of British government and society in that period. By contrast, Henderson was a career diplomat who had consistently supported the official policy of appeasing the Third Reich. On taking up his post in Berlin in 1937, he had pledged that he would seek to see the good as well as the bad in the Nazi regime. To that end he became a good friend of Hermann Göring, who shared his love of hunting. Henderson believed that Hitler was a fact of political life that could not be wished away, but who could be managed if the Western democracies tried to understand his grievances, especially those territorial concessions that had been imposed by the heavy-handed Versailles Settlement. Henderson consistently took the line that Hitler's territorial demands were reasonable. The Czechs had brought about their own fate by refusing to give in to Hitler's initial demands for their German-speaking Sudetenland. Similarly, Germany's demand that the free city of Danzig be returned to the Reich was quite justified in Henderson's opinion, but Poland's anger was not. Naturally, Henderson was outraged by Mason-Mac's plan. It would ignite a major diplomatic crisis at such a delicate moment in European history.

Cold feet at the Foreign Office

Foreign Secretary Lord Halifax, Henderson's boss in London, agreed. The situation in Europe was not so critical as to justify assassination as a substitute for diplomacy, he argued. A personal attack upon Adolf Hitler would be a highly dangerous and inflammatory act and would reflect dishonourably upon Great Britain. Besides, it was 'unsportsmanlike'. Only Sir Stewart Menzies, head of MI6 and like Mason-Mac of Scottish heritage, expressed 'cautious interest' in the idea to decapitate the Third Reich. Mason-Mac was quickly whisked away from Berlin to the promoted post of Brigadier-General, Royal Artillery at Aldershot, where he would have little opportunity to interfere in the great events unfolding in central Europe. As a result, Hitler's parade passed off without bloody interruption. There was no sudden rifle report, no brown-shirted figure slumping to the ground, no panic and hysteria spreading quickly through the city. The Führer's triumph unfolded exactly as its principal designers Albert Speer and Joseph Goebbels had planned. That same day Hitler convened a secret meeting in his study with the senior commanders-in-chief of the Wehrmacht, the Kriegsmarine and the Luftwaffe. He reminded them of the need to wage war while Germany held the initiative. They were ordered to be ready for a lightning war against Poland in the late summer.

8 November 1939
Blowing Up the Bierkeller

The bomb detonated at 9.20 p.m., exactly as planned. Its principal ingredient was Donarit, a gelatinous highly explosive substance used in prospecting and stone quarrying. For good measure, a large quantity of black powder, a quality grade used in mining, was packed around the device. The explosion was as spectacular as the bomber had hoped: the brick and stone column holding the device was obliterated. It had helped support an upper balcony that ran the length of the hall and at the far end of the room the balcony instantly collapsed on to the stage, flattening the small podium that was normally used by speakers. Much of the ceiling collapsed with it. The blast wave rolled out through the hall, shattering the elaborate glass light fittings and blowing out the large windows along the right-hand wall. Even the heavy wooden doors on either side were blown off their hinges. A moment before the bomb went off, the main hall of the Bürgerbräukeller looked much as it had done since its opening in 1885. It was a spacious, well-lit, wood-panelled hall with six long lines of heavy wooden tables covered in white linen and a central aisle leading the eye straight to the stage ahead. Now that stage was invisible, crushed beneath a hideous tangle of broken brick, twisted steel and jagged chunks of demolished concrete. As the cloud of plaster dust settled, it was clear that half of the hall had been reduced to a mountain of rubble, splintered wood and fractured glass.

Flying debris

Only 20 minutes earlier, almost 3,000 people had been crammed into the hall, most sitting at the long tables which were covered in beer mugs. Their jubilant

The Bürgerbräukeller in Munich after the bomb that was designed to eliminate Hitler went off.

cheering, clapping and stamping had itself threatened to bring the roof down. By 9.20 p.m., their meeting over, most of the crowd had sidled out on to Rosenheimerstrasse to make their way home or amble towards another bar. There were only around 120 or so in the hall when their night went horribly wrong. A few of the audience had dawdled in the hall, chatting with old friends and colleagues as they picked up their coats and slowly made for the exit. The bar staff were busy, clearing the tables, collecting the empty glasses and stacking the chairs to make it easier to sweep the floor. Other uniformed staff were taking down the colourful flags and banners that had decorated the hall throughout the evening and a couple of technicians were putting the microphones back in their box. After yet another night of the 'Horst Wessel Song' and *'Der Gute Kamerad'*, the brass band were packing up their instruments and thinking of a beer when a sudden tide of flying debris surged through the room and killed eight people. Several were killed instantly and more than 60 others were injured.

The bomber

Georg Elser had all the technical qualifications needed for the job of bomb maker. He had graduated from training college with excellent grades and was a qualified electrician, as well as being a skilled carpenter and cabinetmaker. After working as a furniture maker he then became a lathe operator, making propellers for the fledgling Dornier aircraft company. When the Great Depression hit Germany, Elser got on his bike and found work wherever he could. In one factory, he made cases for clocks but also learned a great deal about their inner workings. Although a skilled man, he took labouring jobs at the Waldenmaier armaments factory in the industrial town of Heidenheim and at a sloppily-run quarry in nearby Königsbronn. In both of these posts he quickly worked himself up, learned from colleagues and acquired some useful bits and pieces: fuses, detonators, blasting cartridges and a significant supply of explosives. These were needed if he was to fufil his ambition in life: to assassinate Adolf Hitler, Joseph Goebbels and Hermann Göring in one fell swoop.

The quiet man

Elser had several communist friends and colleagues and may have been influenced by them to join the KPD. In the mid-1920s, he seems to have briefly been a member of a militant leftist group, the Red Front Fighters' League. He was certainly a committed trades unionist and a member of the Federation of Woodworker Unions, but he was not particularly interested in leftist politics and was not cut out to be an agitator. A thoughtful but quiet man, he disliked political gatherings and the constant talking and arguing that went on deep into the night. He attended three meetings of the KPD and that was enough. Elser was a practical man of few words. Like many working men in the interwar years, he was only compelled to take an interest in politics thanks to the frustration and despair brought on by periods of unemployment and occasional spells of work in low-paid labouring jobs that made no use of his talents. He did make one important political decision, however. Early on, he decided that he did not like Hitler and his Nazis. He particularly did not like Nazi labour laws and the way they restricted trades unions arguing for a better deal for their members. Throughout the 1930s he kept a note of his ever-falling wages and the ever-rising deductions that Hitler's government took to fund its grandiose schemes.

Although his own private life as a travelling labourer was complicated and featured several women, he had inherited a strong sense of good and evil from his strict Protestant mother. In his own way, he was a moral man and he disliked injustice. He just knew in his bones that the Nazis were a bad lot. In the various small towns where he lived during the Hitler years, he was known to walk away from Nazi demonstrations and parades and he refused to use the Hitler greeting or the Hitler salute. He detested the way in which Hitler had mesmerized the youth of Germany like a modern-day Pied Piper, often alienating them from their parents and families. And he was not taken in by Goebbels' propaganda: he much preferred to listen to the other points of view available on foreign radio stations. A spell at the shipping office in the Waldenmaier armaments works had given him ample evidence of Hitler's preparations for war. In late August 1938, as Europe prepared for conflict over Czechoslovakia, Elser decided that someone had to stop the madman and his gang. If no one else would do it, it would have to be his job.

Best-laid plans

For the next 15 months Elser devoted himself to his plan. He'd realized that the three top Nazis were seldom together in public but they did all attend the annual ceremonies held in Munich every November to commemorate the failed putsch in 1923. Each year a rally for old Party members was held in the Bürgerbräukeller where Hitler had gathered his men and given them a pep talk before marching out to failure and a spell in prison. It was a huge moment in the annual National Socialist calendar. And, Elser noted, the Bürgerbräukeller was a relatively small arena where the impact of an explosion would be particularly lethal.

He made several trips to Munich to find the best spot for secreting a bomb in the ceremonial hall. Finally, he chose a column close to the small platform where Hitler would give his speech and where the other Nazi bigwigs would be sitting. He examined the lower end of the column and measured out where he might create a secret niche that would store the bomb. Elser's parents owned a farm with a small orchard in rural Baden-Württemberg, close to the border with Bavaria, and this provided him with a shed to work in and a secluded spot to test his prototype devices. The bomb was almost ready by early August 1939, so he moved to Munich with his wooden toolbox containing the detonators, some wire, a battery and two Westminster clock movements.

A regular guy

Every day he took an evening meal at the Bürgerbräukeller, getting to know the staff and establishing himself as a pleasant, friendly, regular customer. He was careful to make the acquaintance of the house dog that accompanied the night janitor as he closed up the building and he gave it occasional titbits. It would come to recognize his smell in the hall at night and think nothing of it. Each

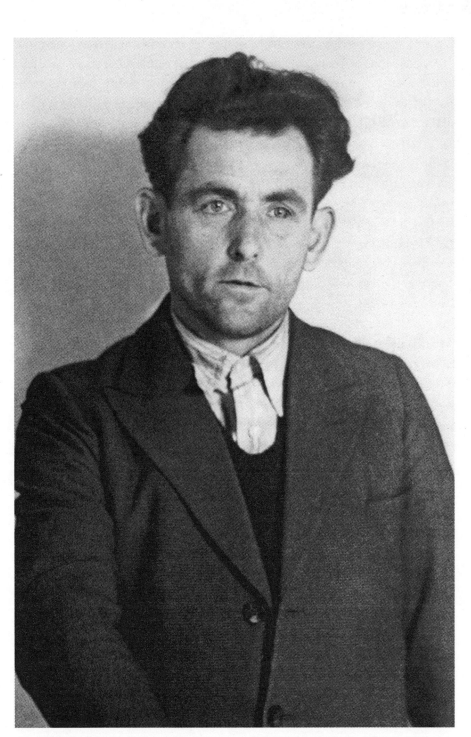

Georg Elser could see the way things were going in Germany and had decided to stop the madman and his gang.

night as closing time approached, he slipped up the stairs to the gallery and hid in a small storeroom until the building closed. Most nights he had at least six hours to get on with his work before the morning kitchen staff started to arrive just before 7 a.m., then it was time for him to slip away out of a side door. If any of the morning staff challenged him, he had practised several excuses to explain his presence, mostly about coming back to retrieve something he had mislaid in the bar the night before. Everything Elser did was meticulously planned and executed. He built a small wooden hinged panel to obscure the incisions that he had to make in the wooden panelling to get access to the column within. And he chose light, sharp tools to drill into the column itself, muffling them to minimize the sound of his activities. As much as possible, he tried to synchronize his blows with noises out in the street and he took exceptional care to cover his tracks in the morning, sweeping up and carrying away any telltale dust and debris he had created.

Setting the date

When the bomb was ready to be inserted into the niche that he had chipped out of the column, it was housed in a well-constructed box packed with cork and wood shavings to mask the ticking of the two clock movements inside. He created a six-day timer to give himself flexibility in deciding when it was safest to take the bomb to the hall, set it and leave it to do its worst. After careful consideration, he placed the bomb in the column niche on Thursday, 2 November and returned three nights later to activate the timer. On the evening of 8 November the Blood Banner of National Socialism would be carried through the packed hall and placed on the stage. A sombre Hitler would follow with bowed head and would then ascend the small podium to address his old comrades. In the column just behind him, Elser's clock-bomb would just about be running out of ticks.

Accidental destiny

Hitler was not having a good week. On Sunday, 5 November his generals had argued yet again that the planned offensive against France should be postponed. Winter was closing in and any military manoeuvres would almost certainly get bogged down. Hitler reckoned that if his generals didn't fancy a winter war, neither would their French and British counterparts. They could, therefore, be caught on the hop. On Tuesday, 7 November he reluctantly agreed to think about the High Command's suggestion of postponing all plans for five weeks and having a new look at the weather forecasts around 12 December. Hitler saw some merit in this: Christmas seemed an even better time to launch a surprise invasion. It was agreed that a final decision on the date for the offensive would be made at a meeting in Berlin on 9 November. But that meant cutting short the annual two-day-long commemoration in Munich of the 1923 Putsch, one of the most cherished highlights in Hitler's year. Reluctantly, the public processions and ceremonies in the heart of the city were cancelled, but the Führer was adamant that his speech to his old warriors at the Bürgerbräukeller on the Wednesday evening should go ahead as usual.

Forecasts of very heavy fog changed Hitler's travel plans, however. His pilots assured him that flying back to Berlin was not advised, so he would have to travel back overnight to Berlin by train. The only feasible slot available for his private train that did not interfere with the other scheduled rail traffic required a 9.31 p.m. departure at the latest. As a result, his grand entry into the Bürgerbräukeller had to begin an hour earlier. His speech was shorter than usual and for once the Führer heeded the signals to shut up that were coming from his nervous adjutants. He wrapped up his speech in record time at 9.07 p.m. and marched smartly out of the hall to a rapturous ovation.

Sadly, the veterans who were there for those special minutes after the speech, when the Führer walked among his old comrades, chatting, shaking hands and acknowledging them as long-remembered friends, would have to be disappointed. Outside, Kempka was ready in the car, waiting to whisk him to the nearby station. Hitler was already in his carriage when Elser's bomb exploded. If the sound of the bomb reached Munich Hauptbahnhof, it was lost in the discordant clangour of a major railway station. The Führer could now relax. He would be back in Berlin in good time for the renewed tussle with his over-cautious generals the following day. The train stopped briefly in Nuremberg and Goebbels took advantage of the halt to send some messages from the stationmaster's office. It was there that he learned of the atrocity back in the beer hall. Hitler's companions were aghast at the news and Eva Braun was especially worried. She had pulled strings for her father to be present at the great event and he was one of the injured. Hitler's first reaction to the news was disbelief and then anger, but later in the journey north he was more bullish about the bomb attack. Once again, he had survived an assassination attempt and both he and his destiny were unscathed.

Caught at the border

On the evening of the Bürgerbräukeller explosion, Georg Elser presented himself at the Swiss–German border near Constance. The guards thought there was something slightly unusual about his manner and decided to search him. In his knapsack they found lengths of wire, a small piece of metal that was later identified as a firing pin, a pencil drawing of a mechanism of some kind and a coloured postcard of the now destroyed beer hall in Munich. Thus began Elser's detention, which would last five and a half years. When questioned, waitresses from the Bürgerbräukeller confirmed that he'd been a regular customer there in recent months. He was a friendly chap who they remembered because he only ordered one small glass of beer each evening. Pus-filled sores on his knees suggested that he'd recently spent a lot of time kneeling: much of Elser's work on the column had been done lower down, near the floor.

The timing of Elser's attempt to cross the border hadn't helped him. He had decided to leave Germany only when he knew that his bomb had worked. Once it had exploded, he knew he couldn't linger in the Reich as the authorities would soon come looking for him. On one of his late-night vigils in the beer hall, a member of staff had found him on the premises long after all the other customers had gone home. He'd prepared a convincing explanation for just such an event but now it would be remembered and would attract suspicion. Under intense Gestapo interrogation, and despite multiple beatings, he stuck to his true story that he had acted alone. He had no collaborators. Not the communists, nor the British, the French or the Jews. Elser hadn't even heard of the Black Front that he was supposed to belong to. He showed his inquisitors five full-scale detailed drawings that he had made of the mechanism. When he was given tools and materials he demonstrated to his captors that he could made a replica of the bomb. At the quarry and the Waldenmaier weapons factory, the Gestapo found plenty of evidence of lax management and poor record keeping. It was obvious to them that Elser could easily have acquired the necessary components to make his bomb. But Hitler refused to believe that this unprepossessing, rather dull man had without substantial support devised and executed a plot that came within a few minutes of wiping out Germany's top leadership, simply because he wanted 'to do something that would prevent further bloodshed'.

Sitzkrieg spies

Within hours of the blast, Georg Elser's failed plot in Munich was bizarrely linked to the wider military situation across Europe. Hitler spent September and October

1939 invading and then subjugating Poland, but nothing much had happened on the Western Front since Britain declared war on 3 September. This standstill was called the Sitzkrieg or sitting war by the Germans, while the phrase Phoney War caught on in Britain and the USA. There were many in the democracies of western Europe, and some in Germany, who hoped that diplomatic action could still help avoid a major conflict. To that end, a relatively minor intelligence operation based in the Netherlands had been under way since early September, involving British and Dutch intelligence. Two British officers, Captain Best and Major Stevens, plus a Dutch agent, Lieutenant Dirk Klop, had taken part in eight secret meetings with a number of allegedly disaffected German officers in different houses across Holland. There was inevitably much deception and shadow-boxing at these events, but in essence the British hoped to identify some genuine oppositionists while the Germans were trawling for any useful information that the British agents might let slip about their other contacts.

Around 9 a.m. on 9 November, 12 hours after the atrocity in Munich, the German agents running their side of the operation received stunning new orders to abduct Best and Stevens. After a shootout at a rail halt on the Dutch–German border near the town of Venlo, the two British Secret Intelligence Service men were bundled into a car and driven off to five and a half years' imprisonment in the Third Reich. Goebbels' propaganda machine left the German people in no doubt that the two spies caught 'fleeing' Germany had been the contacts and handlers of the communist traitor Georg Elser. As 'proof', photographs of the three plotters, Best, Stevens and Elser received equal space on the front pages of Nazi newspapers. In all likelihood, Hitler had simply decided that linking two British spies to the beer hall bombing would help stir up stronger anti-British feeling in Germany.

Later rumours suggested that Elser was receiving 'special prisoner' privileges because someone in the Nazi hierarchy had a reason for keeping him alive. Conspiracy theorists claimed that he had always been working for the SS commander Heinrich Himmler, who planned to kill Hitler and succeed as Führer. However, no convincing explanation has yet been offered to suggest why Himmler would want to sit next to a ticking bomb. Others have claimed that Elser was kept alive because he knew something that Himmler wanted to keep secret. If that had been true, his life in prison would have been over instantly. More likely, Elser was kept in his coop until needed in the future, possibly as a witness in the post-invasion version of the Nuremberg Trials, at which leading British politicians and intelligence figures would be in the dock.

CHAPTER 13

Late 1939

The Phoney War Plots

Hitler was in full rant. Standing and raging at his desk, shaking his clenched fist and spitting out the full menu of scorn, resentment and contempt that he reserved for his senior military commanders. They were timid, frightened, unimaginative cowards and dullards. Not one of them shared or understood his strategic vision. They were all infected with the spirit of Zossen. He would root them all out and replace them with truly heroic commanders who were fit to lead the German army into battle and towards its historic destiny, which was the ultimate victory of the Master Race. On the other side of the table Field Marshal von Brauchitsch, Commander-in-Chief of the Wehrmacht, stood still and endured the barrage. He had expected this tidal wave of invective. Hitler and his generals had been at loggerheads for months. At stake was the decision to end the Phoney War quickly and attack in the west at once.

On a roll

Hitler believed in momentum. Everything had gone as planned in 1939, so it had been a good year. The Western democracies had been paralysed with fear and indecision. In March he had occupied Bohemia and Moravia, snuffing out the hated Czechoslovakia, and as a bonus he had bullied the Lithuanians into handing over the port of Memel or Klaipéda and its hinterland, rubbing out yet another provision of the hated 1919 peace settlement. During the summer he had signed the Pact of Steel with fascist Italy and, more importantly, a non-aggression treaty with the Soviet Union. But the ink was no sooner dry on

the Molotov–Ribbentrop Treaty than Germany invaded western Poland in a lightning war that lasted 36 days. To Hitler, it made sense to press on and maintain the initiative while the gods of war favoured him. Delay would only give the Allies a little more time for preparation before the static war in the west inevitably burst into open conflict.

But his generals disagreed. They lacked his messianic self-belief and could see the difficulties that winter war presented. Few of them had much confidence in Operation Yellow, the plan to invade the neutral Low Countries and France. With the disappearance of Poland in October, Germany now shared a long border with the Soviet Union, a nation that was hardly a reliable or trustworthy ally in their view. As a result, significant German forces were now permanently committed to the defence of the East. France and Britain had been slow to rouse themselves and Hitler had certainly foxed their leaders and diplomats, but they remained powerful foes. The British had their Royal Navy and the French had built a magnificent system of fortifications, far superior to anything else in Europe. There was much to be said for thinking very carefully about Germany's next step. And, as many on the General Staff privately hoped, there might just be another chance to get rid of the mad corporal before Europe erupted into total war.

The veterans of 1938

Many of the plotters from the Czech crisis remained determined to remove Hitler from power. In late summer 1938 they had gained some experience of organizing a clandestine coup and had learned who could be trusted. Their ranks had also grown since the Munich Crisis of September 1938. As Hitler edged Germany ever closer to war throughout 1939, a number of other senior army officers had shown signs that they were sympathetic to the plotters' aims. Most were not convinced that the planned attack in the west would be as easy as Hitler believed. Some had also been disturbed by the terror campaign and mass atrocities against Polish civilians, carried out not only by the SS but by enthusiastic Nazis within the ranks of the Wehrmacht. Oster and Canaris both hoped that the mounting tension throughout the German establishment over the impending escalation of the war in the west would provide them with an opportunity to revive the 'spirit of resistance'. But the tentative, shifting views of General Franz Halder, and the questions he was asking himself, were much more typical of the German top brass in the last weeks of 1939.

Tentative resistance

Halder, who was chief of the Army High Command, disliked Hitler, detested Himmler and believed that the entire Nazi programme was evil. He had considered killing Hitler with his own pistol on several occasions but had failed to act. Oster, Canaris and others felt that Halder had the right moral attributes and the right level of seniority to facilitate action against the Führer. However, like many German officers, Halder could not break the oath of loyalty to Hitler that he had made in 1934, when the Chancellor became the Führer. Then there was his duty to his country. An act against Hitler while Germany was at war was the act of a traitor and a rebel, he felt. Aside from these moral obstacles, there were practical matters to consider. A large number of the army's younger officers had grown up during the Hitler years and many were ardent National Socialists and supporters of the 'Hitler Project'. They would almost certainly be unwilling participants in a coup against the Third Reich.

And what support would there be among the German population at large for a group of relatively unknown generals who assassinated the most popular and successful leader in German history? If Hitler was killed, the Nazi Party would not disappear overnight so would there be any point in killing Hitler if he was merely replaced by Himmler or Göring? From listening to the grapevine, Halder also sensed that the network of potential conspirators in October 1939 was larger than in 1938 but was more scattered and much weaker. When he heard that a new conspiracy was afoot, he moved two tank units to the outskirts of Berlin on the pretext that the machines needed repairs and the men needed rest after the Polish campaign. But now that he saw how unprepared the conspirators were, the tanks were pulled back from the city.

The spirit of Zossen

Halder and Brauchitsch had decided that the best course of action was to try and convince Hitler to postpone the western assault as long as possible. Hitler wanted to attack on 12 November and agreed protocols meant that he should inform the General Staff seven days in advance, to give them time for final preparations. The last opportunity the generals would have to dissuade the Führer from his disastrous course of action would be 5 November, therefore. On that day Brauchitsch and Halder travelled together to present their objections, but in the event Brauchitsch met the Führer and suffered his tirade alone while Halder fretted in the anteroom. The escalation in the west was in fact postponed, but thanks to forecasts of very poor weather rather than any comments that Brauchitsch had made.

Driving away in the car afterwards, he described the 'meeting' to Halder and mentioned Hitler's use of the phrase 'spirit of Zossen'. Since Imperial days this small town in Brandenburg, 20 miles (32 km) south of Berlin, had housed an important military training camp and during the 1930s a large underground headquarters and command centre for the Wehrmacht's highest officers was built there. Hitler had probably used the phrase to sum up the bureaucratic instincts and contemptible inertia of his generals, but Halder wondered if the furious Hitler had unwittingly let slip that he already suspected that staff at Zossen knew about, talked about and were doing something about plans to kill him. Halder was stunned by the thought. At that moment he imagined himself as a victim of the next SS purge and gave up all idea of leading or facilitating any act of resistance.

Hanging up the Führer on the Siegfried Line

After 5 November, Halder's opposition to Hitler was confined to arguing for further postponements of Operation Yellow, while Oster and Canaris seem to have accepted that their best bet now was to play a longer game and wait for bad news in the future. Oster's hatred of Hitlerism had led him to start passing pieces of information to the enemy, but from 1940 onwards both he and Canaris seem to have buckled down to their duties, giving less thought to active conspiracy. There were, however, still some other commanders who were willing to try and do something about Hitler on their own initiative.

General Kurt von Hammerstein-Equord was another German general who had no affection for the Nazis. Hammerstein had been loyal to the Weimar Republic throughout the 14 years of its existence and as far as he was concerned it was a legally constituted government and therefore deserved his obedience. He took little interest in the radical extremist parties that ran amok in Germany in the immediate post-First World War years. After making his way up through the senior ranks thanks to his intelligent planning, which made best use of the limited defence forces that Germany was permitted to have under the Versailles Settlement, Hammerstein became Commander-in-Chief of the Wehrmacht in 1930. He had no affection for Hitler and his Nazis and repeatedly advised President Hindenburg to be very careful in appointing the Austrian demagogue to any ministry in the government. When Hitler became Chancellor, he was required to resign his post.

Hindenburg shielded Hammerstein from Hitler's wrath in the June 1934 purge, or Night of the Long Knives. Hammerstein had, in fact, earlier warned the old president of the coming bloodbath. He was spared but his old friend General von Schleicher was murdered in the purge, as was Schleicher's wife. Army officers were forbidden from attending Schleicher's funeral by order of the new Chancellor, but Hammerstein made a point of turning up at the ceremony. He was then physically escorted away by the SS. After five years' furlough, Hammerstein was briefly reactivated during the invasion of Poland and given temporary command of Army Group A on the northern 'Dutch' stretch of the Westwall. On several occasions, Hammerstein invited the Führer to inspect his troops. It would have been good for their morale, he said, as many of them felt they were missing out on the chance to win glory in the East. And a Führer visit to the Dutch sector would perplex and concern the Allies.

Hitler was suspicious because Hammerstein had never been one of his admirers. In fact, Hammerstein had confided to his retired colleague General Ludwig Beck that he wanted revenge for the death of the Schleichers. If Hitler took up his invitation to visit his troops in the west, he could well meet with a tragic accident, probably involving a live grenade in a concrete bunker that he happened to be inspecting. But Hitler's natural wariness saved him yet again. The Führer was far too busy to visit troops in a holding position on a quiet front, but he found the time to transfer Hammerstein to a demoted post in Silesia and then quickly put him back on the retired list.

Kurt von Hammerstein-Equord died of cancer in April 1943. On his deathbed, he instructed his family to refuse the offer of an official funeral, which was due to an officer of his rank. He did not want his coffin to be draped in the current German national flag, which had a black swastika at its core. And at his private funeral, his family did not display the wreath that arrived from the office of the Führer.

Desperate times

Erich Kordt believed that desperate times called for desperate action. Kordt was an Anglophile who had studied at Oxford and was a diplomat serving in the German Embassy in London. Like many well-educated Germans, he privately detested the Nazis but found it expedient to join the Party in 1937 in order to save his career. In 1938 he was working in Berlin and was very aware of the Oster–Canaris group that hoped to depose Hitler in the wake of a Czech fiasco. Through his brother Theodor, who was also an official at the embassy in

London, he pressed the British to take a defiant position against Hitler over the Sudetenland question. Like Oster and his confederates he was demoralized by Chamberlain's surrender at Munich, which had both doomed Czechoslovakia and raised Hitler's stock within Germany even higher. The obvious potential sources of opposition to Hitler – the Social Democrats, the KPD and the dissidents within the NSDAP – had all long since evaporated and the well-organized attempt at a coup in Berlin had fizzled out. The British and French could not be trusted and even Stalin had signed an agreement with the Nazis. No one seemed able or willing to do anything about the Austrian warmonger.

Suicide mission

On Sunday, 3 September Britain finally but reluctantly declared war on Germany. That day, Kordt was much engaged in discussing the diplomatic ramifications of the news from London with dismayed colleagues. At every private meeting, the same questions emerged: 'Is there any way to stop this war? Can anyone stop Hitler?' It occurred to Kordt that he was better placed than most to come up with an answer. His current post as head of the Ministerial Bureau of the German Foreign Office took him inside the Reich Chancellery on a daily basis. But access to the Führer while he was in Berlin was highly restricted due to the war crisis. The SS were body-searching everyone who had business with Hitler, bar the most senior members of the government, so shooting him with a pistol was out of the question.

Another solution emerged from a discussion with Hans Oster. An attaché case containing explosives might get through if it was made clear to the guards that it contained ultra-sensitive diplomatic documents for the Führer's eyes only. Kordt was willing to take the risk, but he knew that to be sure of killing Hitler he would have to detonate the bomb as close to him as possible. Both men would die in what was a certain suicide mission. Oster promised to supply explosives from the Abwehr arsenal by 11 November, but he was not able to keep the promise. The heightened state of tension meant that the previously easy access to explosives that Abwehr agents had enjoyed was being scrutinized more carefully by the Gestapo. So Kordt was not required to make the ultimate sacrifice. Nor was Hitler.

CHAPTER 14

23 June 1940
An Austrian in Paris

Just before dawn on 23 June 1940, Adolf Hitler's plane touched down at Le Bourget airport. Hitler was about to make his one and only trip to the conquered French capital. The frustrated artist and architect from Linz had come to explore a city he had always dreamed of visiting. He was not there as an all-conquering Caesar in triumph but as an adoring aesthete. His presence in Paris was shrouded in secrecy. He followed his itinerary in a small cavalcade of three black Mercedes saloons, with relatively light security. His companions were not his generals or Nazi potentates but fellow art-lovers, or at least art-lovers who shared his conservative tastes; Arno Breker, the neoclassical sculptor, and his favourite architects Albert Speer and Hermann Giesler. The tourists were photographed at the Eiffel Tower but most of their time in the city was devoted to four buildings that Hitler had long admired and studied in depth: the extravagant Palais Garnier, the Paris opera house, which Hitler thought was 'the most beautiful theatre in the world'; the church of Mary Magdalene, the Madeleine, and the Panthéon, which he thought were sublime reincarnations of ancient Roman architectural values; and the Hôtel des Invalides, which housed the monumental tomb of Napoleon Bonaparte.

At this last stop, Hitler insisted upon being left alone while he stood still for some minutes in front of the imposing sarcophagus of the French dictator. Afterwards he asked his adjutant to remind him to arrange the transfer of the remains of Napoleon's son François from Vienna, to be laid to rest beside his illustrious father. The brief tour ended high up in the artistic village of Montmartre, where the Führer mused on his decision to protect Paris from the full rigours of modern warfare. He had not wanted to be remembered as the vandal who demolished *La Ville Lumière* and his generals had obeyed his wishes. But from this elevated angle, there was much about the city that was clearly muddled and artistically disappointing. Paris would clearly benefit from a dose of Teutonic order in due course. His architects nodded their agreement. By midday, Hitler was back at the Wolf's Gorge, his field headquarters at Brûly-de-Pesche in the Ardennes forests. Over dinner he expressed his belief that Speer would transform Berlin into such an impressive city that Paris would be a mere shadow by comparison. Nevertheless, he hoped to return to Paris in the near future. Those in Hitler's retinue imagined that he was referring to the expected victory parade along the Avenue des Champs-Élysées and through the Arc de Triomphe.

The victory parade

The Führer had attended a magnificent victory parade in Warsaw the previous autumn, on 5 October. He had also made a point of attending the military parade in Memel, when it rejoined the Reich in March 1939. It was only to be expected, therefore, that German troops would celebrate their astonishing victory over France by marching through Paris. No other city in Europe, not even Berlin, offered such an exceptional backdrop for a triumph in the old Roman sense. Several senior commanders had already begun to move units closer to the city, to facilitate the logistics of what was expected to be a spectacular demonstration of German military might. The date for the Paris parade was set for 27 July.

Several German officers took a particular interest in the plans for the parade. In 1940 Erwin von Witzleben commanded the German 1st Army which had broken through the 'impregnable' Maginot Line on 14 June. His reward was the Knight's Cross, the highest military medal in the Third Reich. He was also promoted to the rank of General Field Marshal. Nevertheless, Witzleben was critical of Hitler and sympathetic to the aims of the Oster–Canaris plotters. He had known of Hammerstein-Equord's plan to 'invite' Hitler to the Westwall but had said nothing about it nor done anything to prevent it. Witzleben seems to have been the shield for a plot to shoot Hitler in Paris while he reviewed the victory procession. The assassin was likely to be Count Fritz-Dietlof von der Schulenberg, a government official who had been expelled from the Nazi Party in early 1940. He was judged to be an unenthusiastic supporter of the Party's objectives and therefore untrustworthy. To demonstrate his patriotism,

Erwin von Witzleben was one of the senior officers who demanded an inquiry into the deaths of Schleicher and his friend Ferdinand von Bredow during the Night of the Long Knives, a request that riled the Nazis.

he had instantly volunteered for military service. Although based at Potsdam, he reckoned that in the chaos of a disorganized France he could make his way in uniform to Paris in time for 27 July.

Settling an old score

Two days before Hitler's brief Paris trip, the representatives of France had capitulated and signed an Armistice agreement in the same railway carriage where the Allies had lorded it over the exhausted Germans in 1918. At Hitler's order, Marshal Foch's 'victory' carriage had been taken from its museum to the very spot where the Great War had ended. Hitler sat quietly in Foch's seat and performed a brief Hitler salute when the French officers entered. He left without comment 12 minutes later, once the preamble of the Armistice had been read out by General Keitel. There was no rant and no humiliation of the French delegation. Hitler acted with cold decorum. It was enough for him that the shame of November 1918 had at last been balanced out. The French Republic had already been humiliated enough on the field of battle.

In a mere 46 days, the Wehrmacht had achieved the crushing victory that had eluded the old Imperial army for over four years. France's expensive fortifications had been bypassed and its armies surrounded while French resolve had evaporated at every level. The French had suffered almost 400,000 dead, missing in action or wounded. Over one and a half million French troops had been captured and many were already on their way to labour camps in the Reich. As for the British, they had arrived well prepared and ready to fight the previous war but they had literally been thrown back into the sea. Germany had suffered unexpectedly light casualties, a fact that played very well back home in the Fatherland.

The charm offensive

Master of Europe from the Soviet border to the Atlantic, Hitler was in a mood for reconciliation. There was nothing to be gained from punishing the French nation in defeat. Hitler was keen to convince the French that they would be respected partners in a future fascist Europe. Jews and communists were of course excluded from that offer. German troops in France were strictly warned to behave and not let the Führer down. There would be no looting, no bullying and French women would be treated with respect. By and large the German troops who arrived in Paris that summer behaved well, were happy to have survived the campaign and endeared themselves to the French catering classes by paying for the drinks and meals that they ordered. Many spoke impeccable French and were genuinely keen to explore French culture, history and cuisine. German propaganda films highlighted the Wehrmacht troops handing out water and supplies to stranded refugees on the blocked country roads and helping them turn back towards their homes. Posters with the heading 'Trust the German Soldier!' showed smiling Aryan soldiers feeding abandoned waifs. And there was little need for smart, young, handsome and francophone warriors to force themselves on the local womenfolk. Hitler's charm offensive ensured a calmer atmosphere in Paris than expected, at least during the first few crucial weeks of occupation.

The impromptu parade

Hitler's desire to win over the French people probably explains why there was no grand victory parade through central Paris on 27 July 1940. For Hitler, the Battle of France was already history. He was interested in pacifying the French, not aggravating them. When touring the Great War battlefields in Flanders and Artois on 25 and 26 June, he took care in his comments to treat both the French and German dead with respect. On hearing of a planned victory parade in Paris, Hitler instantly cancelled it. There would be no triumphalism. So there was now no reason for Schulenberg or any other budding assassin to make their way to France that summer. Some German troops did, however, march along the Champs-Élysées in June 1940. Units of the 30th Infantry Division commanded by Kurt von Briesen entered Paris on 14 June and found it undefended, so they staged an impromptu 'parade' through the city on their way southwards to the ever-receding Front. A short piece of film was made of Briesen's men and it was shown over and over again around the world. It was the only footage that a very frustrated Joseph Goebbels had of the historic moment when the Führer captured Paris.

The following summer General Witzleben tried again, this time taking a leaf out of Hammerstein-Equord's book of plots. Like most officers of his rank, Witzleben was aware that the long-dreaded and unwinnable war in the East was not far off. It could only be stopped by killing Hitler. He therefore invited Hitler to take the salute in a parade that he was planning for 21 May 1941. It would be good for the morale of the troops stationed in northern France, and it would give friendly Parisians a chance to see the man who had saved them from Bolshevism and the Jews. By this stage, Hitler was probably just as wary of Witzleben as he had been of Hammerstein two years before.

Even if Hitler had trusted him, he was far too busy to play at parade ground soldiers. Throughout May 1941, Hitler was working with General Jodl and his staff on the finer details of Operation Barbarossa, the surprise attack on the Soviet Union that would hopefully commence at some point in mid-June. And after 10 May he lost time and had to waste energy on minimizing the damage caused by his long-term acolyte Rudolf Hess, who had taken off on a bizarre 'diplomatic' mission to Scotland. His other project that month was the airborne invasion of Crete that was scheduled for 20 May. It got off to a very bad start, although British dithering and poor communications saved his bacon yet again. Hitler had more to worry about than attending another interminable parade and he wondered why Witzleben was suddenly so keen on his presence, so he stayed in Berlin.

1941–43
Plotting on the Roads to Moscow

A t dawn on 4 August 1941 a Focke-Wulf Condor touched down at a small landing strip in north-western Byelorussia. The plane was *Immelmann III*, a specially adapted Fw-200 Condor, registered as D-2600, that Hitler's pilot Hans Baur had recommended to the Führer in 1937. It had a much longer range than his Junkers 52 and with four engines it was safer and better able to carry the heavy armour plating that protected the Führer's personal cabin space. At the edge of the strip, a small convoy of armour-plated cars was waiting to convey Hitler to his destination, the historic town of Borisov, which currently housed the headquarters of the Wehrmacht's Army Group Centre. Borisov was where much of Napoleon's fleeing Grand Army was massacred in 1812 while trying to retreat across the river Berezina. It was now the temporary base for a group of very angry German officers.

Victory in the East!

Six weeks before, on 22 June, the largest invasion force in history launched its surprise attack on the Soviet Union. More than three million German, Finnish, Hungarian, Romanian and Slovak troops took part in Operation Barbarossa. German Army Group North forced its way through the Baltic states towards Leningrad, while Army Group South was to drive deep into Ukraine, towards Kiev and Kharkov. The target for Army Group Centre (AGC) under General von Bock was the Russian capital city. Within 18 days AGC had pushed more than 400 miles (640 km) into Soviet territory and was about to attack Smolensk, the last major city that lay across the main road to Moscow from west to east. By 16 July, and despite desperate Soviet resistance, German troops had taken control of the centre of Smolensk. Some of Bock's advance units had pushed on and were now less than 240 miles (385 km) from Moscow. It seemed quite possible that the German army would be in Moscow before the lime and chestnut trees that lined the city streets in Soviet times began to shed their reddened leaves.

Hitler's orders

On 19 July Hitler signed Directive 33. This diverted many of the motorized and armoured units in AGC to the northern and southern fronts. AGC was stripped of most of its panzers and any further advance on Moscow would have to be undertaken by relatively unsupported infantry. Directive 34 dated 30 July ordered AGC to halt its advance on Moscow and hold its line in the centre. Hitler's gaze had shifted from Red Square to the coalfields of the Donets Basin in Ukraine and the oilfields of Baku in the Caucasus. Cutting Russia off from its primary resources was now Hitler's priority. It made strategic sense. There was also a sound tactical case for slowing the advance on Moscow. AGC's deep advance into USSR territory had been spectacular but also rapid and unexpected, so there was a danger of AGC over-extending itself, with the inevitable supply problems. If it advanced too far east too quickly, it risked creating a bulging salient in the German line that could be exploited by the Red Army.

These were not arguments that convinced the frustrated commanders in Borisov or their military superior back in Berlin, General Franz Halder, the Chief of German High Command. The dissenting officers pointed to the symbolic and logistical importance of Moscow. The Russian capital was the emotional heart of Russia and also the hub of Russia's highly centralized railway network. Losing the city would demoralize the Russian people and disperse their government across various widely scattered regional towns and cities. Occupying Moscow would also give the Wehrmacht the ability to strike out in all directions at a Red Army that would be marginalized and strung out on the periphery. But delaying and weakening the assault on Moscow would only give the Soviets time to recover and regroup. The Führer appreciated the importance of this disagreement and arranged to travel to Borisov to explain his decision in person and ensure that his orders were fully understood and carried out.

No saint but no Nazi

Major General Henning von Tresckow was a decorated Great War hero and an intelligent man from a Prussian family of impeccable pedigree and military renown. After the war he travelled extensively, working as an international

A strategic meeting of army officers during 1940 including Henning von Tresckow (fourth from the right) and Fabian von Schlabrendorff (far right in glasses).

banker. He spoke several languages well and understood and appreciated other cultures. Eventually returning to the army, he graduated from the General Staff Academy as top student in his year in 1936. However, even as the frenzied crowds scattered flowers at the Führer's feet in the golden years from 1938 to 1941, Tresckow never signed up to Project Hitler. Deeply read in military history and strategy, he was convinced that Germany lacked the material resources to maintain a prolonged war against numerous foes.

Tresckow was an effective and therefore ruthless soldier and officer, so he was no saint. Nevertheless, he was appalled by the atrocities committed by the SS *Einsatzgruppen* against the civilian populations of occupied Poland and Russia and their elimination of thousands of Soviet prisoners of war. Like other men of his background and experience, he believed that the sooner Hitler was removed the better for Germany. One of those co-believers was Tresckow's adjutant, Fabian von Schlabrendorff, also an aristocrat. Schlabrendorff was already acting as a channel of communication between Tresckow and other well-placed oppositionists such as Hans Oster and Witzleben. Both men realized that Hitler's journey to Borisov offered an opportunity to act on their principles and they resolved to shoot the Führer at some point in his visit. They would simply stand smartly to attention as Hitler arrived, calmly withdraw their pistols and gun him down. One of them was sure to get him.

The wary warlord

They reckoned without Hitler's natural wariness. He refused the offer of a General Staff motor car to collect him from the landing strip and convey him the two miles or so to AGC headquarters: he had little confidence in Wehrmacht security and feared a bomb. Instead, Himmler had been ordered to provide a

substantial SS guard at the airstrip and ensure that a fully SS-checked vehicle was waiting for him on the tarmac. Tresckow and Schlabrendorff were armed and ready to dispose of the Führer but they barely glimpsed him as he was quickly hustled into the HQ, surrounded on all sides by his black-clad minders. Only generals Beck and Guderian were allowed into the room to meet the Führer. Even the very senior Major General Tresckow was barred by the SS. Hitler departed as quickly, as furtively and as safely as he had arrived. Tresckow was disappointed but not discouraged. There would be other opportunities to kill Hitler but a more devious stratagem would obviously be required. Tresckow and Schlabrendorff would have to wait 20 months for a second chance to execute Hitler, but when it arrived they would be better prepared.

Plots on all fronts

It was clear to Tresckow that Hitler fully understood that he had many potential foes within the Wehrmacht and that he realized he would always have to be on his guard when on army territory. Tresckow was right. By late 1941, Hitler was very well aware that the upper ranks of the military were stocked with men who did not just disagree with his plans and decisions: many officers had personal, political and/or strategic reasons for loathing him. In early December Hitler visited the HQ of Army Group South (AGS) at Zhdanov, now Mariupol, on the Sea of Azov. Hitler was noticeably ill at ease throughout his entire time there. Something at Zhdanov didn't seem right and Hitler's strong sense of self-preservation kicked in yet again. He was right to be suspicious. Some AGS officers were planning to finish him and his wretched war. Generals Lanz and Speidel and the senior tank commander in the Group, Colonel Graf von Strachwitz, had the same idea as their colleagues further north in Smolensk. They planned to act when Hitler visited AGS HQ in early March 1943, then at Poltava in central Ukraine. In the event, Hitler decided to fly on south, closer to the Front near Zaporizhia on the Dnieper, and thus swerved the bullet yet again. It was a sign that Hitler no longer trusted his officers. Taking off from Zhdanov in December 1941, he had confided in his valet Heinz Linge: 'I'm glad that you are sitting behind me Linge, rather than some Gruppenführer who would shoot me in the back.'

Weary and weakened

Spotted in the clear skies above Smolensk on 13 March 1943, coming in to land from the south, were three large Condors guarded by a detachment of

Messerschmitt 109 fighters. This close to the Front, air cover was definitely needed: in late 1942 Soviet fighters had come close enough to leave a few bullet-holes in the wing of Hitler's aeroplane. At Smolensk airstrip, Hitler and his aides emerged from the first Condor while the other two planes discharged his private security squad: SS Leibstandarte men bearing sub-machine guns. The old days of light security around the Führer had long gone, as had the air of invincibility that he once radiated. Germany had been at war with the USSR for almost 21 months and the early euphoria of summer 1941 had long since evaporated. The dream of an autumn stroll through the Tainitski gardens in the Kremlin had faded. Moscow had not fallen in the first autumn, nor the second, and the depleted Afrika Korps was now holed up in Tunisia, only weeks away from inevitable surrender. Massive preparations were under way for the Allied invasion of Italy, Germany had lost an army at Stalingrad and Hitler had lost much of his credibility as an invincible warlord. It was a chastened, ageing and tired Führer who stepped down on to the strip at AGC HQ.

The bunkered Führer

Hitler was returning from Werwolf, the most easterly and isolated of the bases that he actually used, deep inside Ukraine near the city of Vinnytsia on the river Bug. His flight destination was Wolfsschanze, Wolf's Lair, his main headquarters, on the Eastern Front near Rastenburg in East Prussia. From the first days of Operation Barbarossa in June 1941 until November 1944, this was effectively Hitler's home. He was seldom seen in public now in Germany and his spells at the Berghof were fewer and often enforced by his doctors. Many of his public duties in the Fatherland were undertaken by Goebbels while most of his waking hours were spent underground in concrete bunkers along the Russian Front. The brief stop at Smolensk was arranged to give Hitler an opportunity to meet in private with Field Marshal von Kluge. He had replaced Bock as commander of Army Group Centre after Bock's failure to capture Moscow in late 1941. On the agenda was Operation Zitadelle, a massive German panzer counter-offensive in the crucial Kursk salient. It was planned for May but was already running late. In the event, it launched in July.

Hitler met Kluge and Tresckow as he stepped down on to the tarmac but once again he was encircled by alert and heavily armed SS guards. Kluge offered his staff car to the Führer for the short transfer to his HQ and again the offer was refused. Hitler's trusted chauffeur Erich Kempka had driven a safe car all the way from Germany to Smolensk, just to carry his boss the few kilometres from the airstrip and back. At AGC HQ, Kluge and Hitler met in secret. Kluge expressed his concerns about the preparations for the Kursk offensive but Hitler dismissed them. The two men then had a meal with a small group of Kluge's senior colleagues and Hitler's companions: several staff officers, his personal adjutants, a secretary, the official photographer and his preferred physician of the moment, the obese and sinister Dr Morell. Lunch over, all departed for the airstrip, where Hitler boarded his plane and set off again for Rastenburg. Only one thing was different now. There was a powerful bomb on Hitler's plane, which was timed to explode 30 minutes after take-off, when the Führer would be somewhere over the ancient Polotskian city of Minsk.

Bullet or bomb?

Tresckow and Schlabrendorff learned of Hitler's brief stopover in Smolensk in advance. They had been thinking of how best to use an opportunity such as this for some time. There was little point in trying to shoot Hitler as he either entered or left the AGC HQ building, or when he took lunch with Kluge. He would just be too well-guarded. Kluge might also be hit by the gunfire and he was needed to calm the army when the news broke. It was possible to position experienced and 'reliable' riflemen at various points between the airstrip and the HQ but there was a distinct danger that they would get embroiled in a gunfight with the SS guards. And a bloodbath could spark similar conflicts between regular Wehrmacht troops and the SS along the Front. In any case, it was possible that Kempka, who understood Hitler's long-standing fear of ambush, would take an unexpected route and avoid any waiting snipers.

A bomb had several advantages over the bullet, especially one detonated far from AGC HQ. If Hitler's plane crashed as a result of a bomb explosion, it could take time to find the wreckage, examine it and establish the actual cause of the 'accident'. Not least, a reasonably long period might elapse before the identity of the perpetrators of the plot was discovered. These potential delays, and the public shock that would be generated by the sudden death of the Führer, might hopefully create an atmosphere that would encourage the fall of the regime and the end of the war. The difficulty was getting the bomb on to Hitler's plane.

Danke, Kamerad

Tresckow and Schlabrendorff had given the problem much thought and had come up with a possible, but highly risky, solution. On the day, they carried out their plan to perfection. At lunch, Major General von Tresckow had casually chatted with one of Hitler's staff officers, Colonel Heinz Brandt. Could Brandt do him a small favour, he asked. He had two bottles of quality cognac. They were for a friend at HQ High Command, Major General Hellmuth Stieff, and were part gift and part payment for a small lost wager. Could Brandt pass them to Stieff's adjutant on his behalf? He didn't want to send them through the normal channels as they would take weeks to get there, if they weren't stolen or smashed in transit. Of course, Brandt was happy to help a senior officer. As he boarded the plane for East Prussia, Lieutenant Schlabrendorff stepped forward, handed the packaged bottles into his safe custody, and passed on Tresckow's thanks for helping him out.

Full strength brandy

The job of sourcing a suitable explosive had been taken on by one of Tresckow's friends, Rudolf Christoph von Gersdorff, an aristocrat and an Abwehr officer within Army Group Centre. By 1943, the procedures for requisitioning explosives from Wehrmacht and Abwehr magazines had been tightened up and they were now meant to be monitored by the Gestapo. Fortunately, Gersdorff learned that the Abwehr also stored a quantity of British plastic explosive known as Composition C, which was often used by British SOE agents or supplied to partisan groups within Europe by parachute drop. It would seem perfectly reasonable for an intelligence officer involved in counter-partisan activities to express an interest in an enemy weapon. Gersdorff was therefore able to build up a small supply of 'plastic C' and learned to respect its exceptional explosive power. In a demonstration arranged for Gersdorff and some junior Abwehr officers, a very small quantity blew the turret off an abandoned Soviet tank. It would certainly be strong enough to obliterate the steel panels that defended Hitler from enemy attack in the air.

The finishing touches

The detonation of the bomb depended on a slim tube that contained a copper chloride solution, which would react with and corrode a thin piece of aluminium wire that prevented the firing pin from thrusting down on to the percussion cap. This gave the bombers two crucial advantages. The copper chloride took a little time to dissolve the wire, so Hitler would be many thousands of feet in the air before it completed its job. And this chemical approach to detonation was silent and odour-free. There was no need for a noisy clockwork mechanism and no smell from a slow-burning fuse. The Composition C was carefully shaped to resemble bottles of cognac and then immaculately wrapped in layers of gift paper tied up with coloured cord.

Schlabrendorff watched the Condor take off northwards and returned to AGC HQ to wait for the inevitable radio messages: the Führer's plane was mysteriously delayed. The Führer's plane was missing, possibly shot down by Soviet fighters. Then the confirmation by the landing Messerschmitt pilots that the Condor had exploded in mid-air at high altitude. There was no hope of survivors.

But the message that did arrive at Smolensk was a simple terrifying one-line report that Hitler had landed safely at Rastenburg.

Schlabrendorff's sangfroid

There was no time for expressions of disappointment or recrimination. The plotters now had a serious problem. They had known all along that if anything went wrong, all fingers instantly pointed in their direction. Had the SS men on board Hitler's plane decided to open the package? If so, the plotters were all dead men. On the other hand, if the package was already on its way to Stieff's office and was opened, everyone connected with it would soon be swept up by the SS. It would be open season upon any Wehrmacht officer who was remotely suspected of conspiracy or oppositionist tendencies. Showing great presence of mind, Schlabrendorff quickly telephoned Brandt's office and apologized profusely for handing over the wrong gift to the colonel. His boss was furious with him. Schlabrendorff was due to fly up to Rastenburg on the regular courier plane later in the day. Could they please hang on to the package and he'd bring the correct gift with him?

Later examination suggested that the corrosive solution and the plastic explosive had been affected by the low temperature during the high-altitude flight. The early version of plastic C that was used hardened at approximately minus 40 degrees and the cupric solution may also have frozen. Colonel Brandt had obviously put the cognac in the luggage hold rather than taking it into the heated cabin. Another chance to annihilate Hitler had passed but Schlabrendorff's quick thinking and bravery had not just saved the lives of the plotters at AGC HQ. If the Gestapo had interrogated the resistance officers at Smolensk, they would almost certainly have rolled up the entire framework of opposition within the Wehrmacht.

CHAPTER 16

21 March 1943

The Exhibition Bombers

Heroes' Memorial Day was a highlight in the Nazi calendar. Since 1871 a special day had been set aside to commemorate those who had died in the wars against Denmark, Austria and France that led to Germany's unification. After the Great War, Germany's huge losses were also remembered on this day of national mourning. These were moments of personal and collective sadness and they were usually religious in character. They were normally led by priests and pastors in churches, in churchyards, in parks or at the corner of a town square, wherever a plaque or monument to the local dead had been raised. Local and national flags flew at half-mast.

That all changed in 1934 when *Heldengedenktag* was Nazified and militarized. The purpose of the day was no longer to lament the loss of the fallen but to salute German military history and strength. Quiet reflection was replaced by brash parades and flags were flown at full mast by order. Speeches at local events were now delivered by local Party leaders and military officers, and their content was specified by Goebbels' Ministry of Propaganda so that they emphasized military and diplomatic themes of current significance. The most important speech of the day was given by Hitler in Berlin. It was obligatory for all Germans to listen to the live radio broadcast. In 1943 one of Hitler's commitments on this national holiday was to speak at an exhibition in the Berlin Zeughaus, the old Prussian Arsenal or Armoury.

A temple to Mars

The baroque Zeughaus palace on Unter den Linden in the heart of the city was one of the most imposing structures in Berlin. While other great palaces of that age celebrated the arts, the Zeughaus was a shrine to the god of war. Built by Frederick I of Prussia, it was established to reflect his interest in weapons and martial paraphernalia. It had become an official military museum in Bismarck's time as Chancellor.

On Heroes' Day, 21 March 1943, Hitler was scheduled to visit the Armoury, give a short speech and then visit an exhibition of captured Soviet weapons and insignia. On similar occasions, the Führer had always shown a very deep and genuine interest in foreign weaponry, asking detailed questions of his guides and clearly seeking to identify any possible features that could be adopted by German manufacturers.

As most of the exhibits on show had been captured by Army Group Centre, Colonel Rudolf Christoph Freiherr von Gersdorff was selected to act as Hitler's personal guide. He qualified for the role on a number of grounds. A Silesian aristocrat, he was connected through his first marriage to the wealthy Kramsta industrial family and through his second he was connected to the Prussian royal family. Not only was he a suitable chap to meet and converse with the Führer but he was also an active officer in AGC, who could explain the tactical battlefield contexts in which the weaponry had been deployed and captured. He was also, of course, a good friend of those indefatigable plotters Tresckow and Schlabrendorff.

Gersdorff's plan

All three AGC officers had identified Heroes' Day as the ideal moment to make another attempt at eliminating Hitler. To all three men, the very perversion of a day of sacred remembrance into one of militaristic bombast exemplified the evil at the heart of the Nazi regime. Schlabrendorff undertook to furnish a suitable explosive device by 21 March while Gersdorff was the ideal hitman, as he had an official reason to be part of Hitler's inner group on the day. Gersdorff arrived in Berlin on 19 March and on the pretext of doing his homework for his forthcoming duties he visited the Armoury to examine the atrium and the exhibition gallery, seeking to identify suitable locations for the bomb. He quickly realized that given the layout of the rooms and the level of security surrounding the occasion, placing a bomb in an undetectable location on the day and setting its timer would be difficult and would likely be ineffective. Like Erich Kordt four years before, he acknowledged that to be sure of killing Hitler he would have to carry the bomb close to the Führer's person at the very moment of explosion. Gersdorff was on a suicide mission.

Ten minutes to freedom

On 20 March Schlabrendorff arrived in Berlin with two small devices, which probably contained some of the unused 'cognac' from eight days before. These would easily fit into the deep pockets of Gersdorff's service greatcoat. He would not look out of place in such a heavy, functional garment, as the audience in the Armoury would be largely composed of officers from the three armed services and most would be wearing official coats. It was still March, wartime Berlin was cold and like many museums the old Zeughaus was very poorly heated. The two friends quickly discussed Gersdorff's decision to sacrifice himself for the good of Germany and then spent time examining the range of fuses that Schlabrendorff had brought. Gersdorff selected a standard ten-minute fuse of a type known for its reliability. As Hitler's technical guide for the event, he knew that only ten minutes had been allotted for the Führer's opening speech and a further ten minutes for his tour of the exhibition. This was far less than the two plotters had expected, but Hitler had many other important public commitments to squeeze into that special day. Gersdorff would set the timer once the speech was over and as Hitler entered the exhibition gallery. Even if there were unforeseen problems, he would have a full ten minutes to get close enough to the Führer to be sure of killing him. His wristwatch would tell him exactly when to step forward, clench Hitler tightly to his own body and blow him to pieces.

Thank you, my friend

Hitler's morning on 21 March was spent bestowing medals on the current crop of great Germanic heroes. The little Austrian corporal enjoyed these routine but necessary duties immensely, as they had once been the task of the Kaiser. The highlight of the morning had been the award of the Knight's Cross with Oak Leaves to his dear friend Josef 'Sepp' Dietrich. He was a genuinely close friend of the Führer and one of the few who could speak honestly to him without fear of retribution. From chauffeur and bodyguard Dietrich had risen to Oberst-Gruppenführer, the most senior rank in the paramilitary Waffen-SS. His gong was a reward for his contribution to the bloody recapture of Kharkov in late February and early March. With that pleasant duty accomplished, Hitler set off for what promised to be an interesting visit to the Zeughaus museum.

A whirlwind visit

He arrived at the Zeughaus a little after noon. His ten-minute talk overran by four minutes but by Hitler's standards that was punctuality and self-discipline indeed. Perhaps he was feeling the chill in the high-ceilinged entrance hall of the palace. Throughout Hitler's speech Gersdorff stood at the entrance to the gallery which contained the Soviet weaponry. As Hitler stepped down from the small podium and walked towards him, Gersdorff pressed the timer for the device in his left-hand side pocket. He assumed that activating one bomb would be enough, as the blast of one would ignite the other. There was now exactly ten minutes in which to get close enough to the Führer to take both their lives.

To Gersdorff's surprise, however, the adjutants flanking Hitler failed to introduce him as Hitler's personal technical guide, ready to answer any questions he might have about the exhibits. The Führer himself walked straight past and through into the gallery as if something had already caught his attention. He was followed by the inevitable gaggle of courtiers in pursuit of their leader. It took Gersdorff more than a minute to make his way forward to a point where he could attempt to draw Hitler's attention to a particularly interesting feature. At that point he was in competition with Göring, who had also seen something that he thought the Führer would find fascinating. Hitler ignored both of them. He stopped, scanned the assembled exhibits in the gallery, turned and promptly made for the exit.

A frantic fumble

For reasons of his own, he had truncated his ten-minute visit to under two. SS Leibstandarte guards stepped forward to bar others from following the Führer as he hastily made his way to the waiting car. Yet again, a sudden unexpected change of plan had carried Adolf Hitler out of danger. Gersdorff had failed as others had done. His despair at missing the chance to kill Hitler turned to panic and horror as he remembered that he had enough live explosive in his pockets to blow up most of the exhibits in the gallery. Ten minutes of fuse time was running down fast. His survival was only due to the proximity of one of the museum's toilets, where a terrified Gersdorff successfully deactivated the device in his pocket. He had narrowly avoided becoming the only victim of Schlabrendorff's plastic explosive.

Hitler's fashion parade

On 16 November 1943 Hitler was scheduled to attend a fashion parade of sorts. In fact, he had gone out of his way to ensure he was present at the event by ordering that it be held, not in Berlin, but at Wolf's Lair, his East Prussian bunker complex. Hitler had not suddenly developed a passion for haute couture. His interest in the clothes being modelled on that day was a critical matter for his reputation and that of the Nazi government. In late 1941, the Wehrmacht had been caught out by the onset of the coldest Russian winter in recorded history. Vehicles had frozen solid and become entrapped in snow and ice because of a lack of suitable antifreeze and lubricants. Supplies of feed for the many hundreds of thousands of horses that the Wehrmacht still depended upon failed to reach the Front. And troops in light summer issue uniforms suffered horrific injuries from frostbite. An Italian journalist in Warsaw described the arrival of damaged men returning from the Front, their faces deformed by the onslaught of General Winter. Many had lost noses, ears, lips and eyelids and some had also lost feet, fingers and genitals, thanks to the bitter and unending frost.

The Wehrmacht had fallen victim to its own success earlier in the year. By December, the Front was a long way from the Fatherland. There were piles of winter supplies for men, machines and horses sitting in Poland but there was no easy way to get them to the men in distant front-line positions. The Russian roads had been washed away in an unexpectedly wet autumn *rasputitsa* or rainy season, which had turned much of western Russia into a quagmire. In addition, German engineers struggled to adapt German rolling stock to fit the idiosyncratic gauge used by Russian railways. Dropping supplies by air in dreadful conditions, another alternative, had its own drawbacks. Accurate drops signalled the position of German units to the enemy while inaccurate drops often resulted in food and weapons being spirited away by Russian partisans.

The Führer's fault

Goebbels' Ministry of Propaganda tried to put a positive spin on the logistical disaster that had brought the Eastern offensive to a sudden, shivering halt. German cinema newsreels portrayed cheery *Kameraden* enjoying a swig of schnapps in their snowy foxholes. But there were too many German families with menfolk fighting in Russia to cover up the chaos. The German public were shocked and angry at the lack of planning by their leaders and many knew that the Führer shared a good part of the blame. In modern parlance, Hitler was a climate-change denier. He likened meteorological scientists to the fraudulent alchemists and astrologers of earlier times, openly mocking Wehrmacht officers who took weather conditions into account when planning their campaign strategy. As a result of his scorn for 'that crowd at Zossen' he had not listened to their requests that more thought should be given to the needs of the army if the war dragged on into winter. Hitler chided his defeatist generals: he trusted his men to battle through to Moscow before winter set in. It was only a little bad weather and members of the Master Race could cope with that. He liked to remind listeners that he only wore long trousers when it was required by protocol. When he eventually retired to Linz, as a true Aryan man he would wear only lederhosen and shorts, especially in the coldest depths of winter. That mixture of scorn and over-confidence contributed to the death of countless Wehrmacht soldiers and scarred thousands of others.

Convincing the sceptics

In the following winter, the army was better clad and better supplied but public confidence in Hitler and his regime on this particular matter was not restored. It was vital that Hitler be seen to be taking all steps possible to ensure that the troops on the Eastern Front were fully equipped for their third winter in Russia. Taking advice from Finnish advisers, new winter uniforms were designed for the Wehrmacht, the Waffen-SS and the Luftwaffe Field Divisions. On 16 November, Hitler would be filmed taking a keen interest in these new uniforms at his East Prussian HQ, Wolfsschanze. The soldiers chosen to model the new garb were selected for their height, physique and 'typically Germanic' facial features. One of them was Baron Axel von dem Bussche-Streithorst.

An officer and a gentleman of the 9th

Oberleutnant, later Major, von dem Bussche served with the elite 9th Infantry Regiment. Garrisoned at the army's spiritual home of Potsdam and arguably the most historic unit in the German army, it was certainly the most socially elevated. It was often derided by troops in more humble units as *Infanterie-Regiment von Neun* or just *Graf Neun*, a reference to the number of aristocrats within its ranks. At least 21 officers of the 9th are known to have taken part in some way in anti-Hitler plotting. Von dem Bussche's personal opposition to the Nazi Reich was confirmed in 1942, when he came upon an *Einsatzgruppe* at work in the western Ukrainian city of Dubno. More than 12,000 Jews from the city and its hinterland had been gathered into two ghettos and they were now being machine-gunned before tumbling into the pits that they had been forced to dig. That day von dem Bussche swore to kill Hitler. His selection for the winter uniforms exhibition gave him an unexpected opportunity to penetrate Hitler's security and his plan was as simple as Gersdorff's eight months earlier. Parts from a grenade were used to construct a device with a four-second fuse that could be carried unnoticed within the deep pockets of either his greatcoat or his field trousers. As Hitler closed in to admire the detail of his winter cladding, von dem Bussche would grasp the monster and carry him off to hell.

This time it was the RAF that came to Hitler's rescue. The day before the show, the uniforms were in transit to Wolf's Lair in a railway goods wagon east of Berlin, but RAF bombers spoiled Hitler's fashion party by blowing the train and its contents to shreds. A new date of 11 February was planned for the uniform inspection but by then von dem Bussche had lost part of a leg in action and no longer looked the part for Goebbels' film shoot. Fellow officer and plotter Ewald von Kleist, son of the oppositionist lawyer, offered to stand in for von dem Bussche and put his bomb to good use. However, a successful Russian advance in the Baltic sector and the Allied landings at Anzio and Nettuno alarmed the Führer and diverted his attention. Several new dates for the uniform parade were pencilled into Hitler's diary and then rubbed out, but the winter fashion movie was never shot.

11 March 1944
Back to the Berghof

O n 8 March 1944 Hitler finally accepted that Germany did not have the men or the materiel to continue fighting an offensive war against the Soviet Union. It was a critical moment in the Second World War. In the previous summer the massive German panzer attack in the Kursk salient had failed, resulting in heavy losses of experienced men and of weaponry which was becoming more and more difficult to replace. Much of Germany's industrial infrastructure had been damaged by Allied bombing and parts for replacement tanks and planes as well as for the new miracle weapon, the V1 rocket, were increasingly being made in underground factories using slave labour. In Italy, the advancing Allied forces that had been held back at Monte Cassino since 17 January were now on the verge of a major breakthrough, less than 90 miles (145 km) south of Rome. There would almost certainly be Allied landings somewhere in north-west Europe in the coming summer. The war was inevitably turning against Hitler, who now believed that in order to fight successfully on all fronts Germany needed to adopt a new defensive approach. His rhetoric had taken on a distinctly negative tone in recent months. He no longer spoke of blitzkrieg but of defending the Fatherland to the last breath, resisting Germany's foes to the last bullet and tackling them at the last barricade with knives and fists if need be.

Backs to the wall

Hitler planned to call the senior commanders in the Wehrmacht, the Luftwaffe and the Kriegsmarine to a special conference at the Berghof on 11 March. There he would confirm that he was satisfied that the Atlantic Wall, the concrete fortifications and artillery batteries along the coast of western Europe and Scandinavia, was sufficiently robust and well enough manned to deal with the expected landings there later in the year. And if the Allies broke through south of Rome, preparations were well in hand for new defensive lines in northern Lazio, Umbria and Tuscany. The problem was the almost 1,400-mile-long (2,250 km) Eastern Front. Hitler would reveal his solution on 11 March: the army would be concentrated in a chain of heavily fortified strongpoints and 'Fortress Cities' stretching from Reval, or Tallinn, in the Baltic to Crimea in the Black Sea. These sites would be made impregnable but German forces would be able to sally out from them and hit the Red Army in its flanks. It was in essence the strategy of defensive immobility that had failed France in 1940: the very antithesis of the war of fast movement, the lightning war, that had won Hitler victories in 1939 and 1940. This was a clear sign that Hitler knew that the war was no longer winnable. The best he could hope for now was a stalemate.

The Berghof conference

On 10 and 11 March, Salzburg airport and the landing strip at Obersalzberg were both busy as commanders flew in from around the Reich for the hastily called conference. A Condor from Hitler's own fleet had been sent for one of the key men in his new plan, Field Marshal Ernst Busch, who had been Commander-in-Chief of Army Group Centre at the heart of the Russian Front since the previous October. He was accompanied by his aide Eberhard von Breitenbuch, who held the rank of Rittmeister or Cavalry Master. Like almost all German officers, whether loyal or dissident, Breitenbuch knew that the war was lost. He also knew that Hitler would never accept President Roosevelt's Casablanca demand that only an unconditional German surrender was acceptable. Hitler would fight until the last drop of German blood spilled on to the bomb-shattered pavements of central Berlin, so he would therefore have to be eliminated if Germany was to have peace. Breitenbuch was a protégé and friend of Major General Tresckow. He was also a crack shot and was carrying a loaded pistol. Hitler's would-be assassin didn't expect to be boarding the Condor on its return flight to Byelorussia.

In the hall of the mountain Führer

The meeting was to be held in the Great Hall at the Berghof. On its lower level, it comfortably held enough chairs for an audience of 60 or 70. Three marble steps led up to a smaller raised level dominated by a vast fireplace in dark red marble and heavy wooden furniture in an 'ancient Teutonic' style, designed to evoke a mythological Wagnerian atmosphere. In normal circumstances, the setting would have been completed by a large rotating globe, a slightly smaller version of the one in the Berlin Chancellery that Charlie Chaplin had famously copied to stunning comic effect in his film *The Great Dictator*. However, given the increasing likelihood of an Allied air attack, many of the props of leadership that were usually on display in the hall – the massive furniture, the books and the paintings – had been cleared away to the other, more functional Berghof that operated deep underground. As the war had crept closer to the homeland, the Berghof's 'manager', Martin Bormann, had supervised the construction of an intricate network of subterranean rooms and tunnels. If enemy aircraft were spotted in the Alpine skies, the important guests would be able to retire and continue their meeting in safety below. The garrison of SS Leibstandarte guards was on full alert, as were the teams that manned the battery of anti-aircraft guns deployed throughout the Obersalzberg valley. The only threat to Hitler that hadn't been planned for was the 34-year-old cavalry officer who was striding directly towards the door that led into the conference hall.

Special order by the Führer

Breitenbuch had discussed his tactics with Tresckow and other dissidents. He had been offered a bomb but had decided against using it. At the Berghof, it would look distinctly odd and suspicious if he approached the Great Hall wearing a field overcoat. The drill for visiting officers at Hitler's mountain court was by now well known. On arrival at the complex, he would be led to one of the service buildings for guests and taken to its underground canteen for refreshments. At that point, an orderly would take his outerwear and check it in. Then, like the other guests, he would make his way to the central building by tunnel, dressed in his field jacket. Unfortunately, none of his pockets would now be deep enough for concealing a bomb. Moreover, the SS Leibstandarte guards at the Berghof were not just devoted to their leader but were known for carrying out their duties in a highly professional manner, so he expected to be frisked thoroughly. However, the guards would not look askance at a small pistol in his possession. In fact, it might seem more curious to them if a serving officer was not armed while on duty. And as Breitenbuch assured his colleagues, he was usually a cool fellow under pressure and a rather good shot. He could plug two, maybe three, bullets into Hitler's skull before his minders had even begun to react.

At first all went as Breitenbuch had predicted. The preliminaries over, he and Field Marshal Busch emerged from the tunnel and made their way to the entrance of the conference hall. At that point, an SS officer stepped forward and detained Breitenbuch by the arm: 'Officers below the rank of general are not permitted to enter the conference chamber today. Please wait in the anteroom or outside the House. Special order from the Führer.' There was no point in resisting or attempting to brush past the guards. He would have been taken out in seconds, in both senses of the phrase. Once again, a sudden decision by Hitler had foiled a plot to kill him. Busch then went ahead alone while Breitenbuch was left kicking his heels in the entrance to the Führer's Alpine villa. At least he had the compensation of admiring the collection of rare mountain plants and cacti from around the world that Eva Braun and her sister Gretl had been carefully curating in the Berghof's vestibule.

A regular visitor to the Berghof

One other Wehrmacht officer would have an opportunity to kill Hitler in the Obersalzberg in the summer of 1944. Between 7 June and 11 July 1944, he would be in Hitler's presence three times at the Berghof. At the first meeting his briefcase only contained some relevant papers, but on the next two occasions it contained a powerful explosive device. And yet he did not press the trigger. He had decided that he would eventually detonate the British plastic explosive that he was carrying around with him, but not at the Führer's holiday home in beautiful Bavaria. Instead, he would liquidate Hitler once and for all at Wolf's Lair, his East Prussian HQ near Rastenburg. The officer's name was Colonel Claus Graf von Stauffenberg.

A British attack on the Führer?

Within two weeks of the Fall of France in June 1940, British commanders were giving serious thought to killing Hitler. Initially the plan was to disrupt the inevitable victory parade that the Nazis would stage in central Paris. Officers who knew Paris well from happier days were invited to consider the most likely position for the Führer's podium, taking Gestapo security concerns and Goebbels' publicity demands into account. They agreed that on the big day Hitler would probably be close to the Arc de Triomphe, an ideal location in which to salute his men and an equally perfect setting for a low-level RAF bombing run. But the idea was quietly dropped. Goebbels' cameras would certainly be covering the event and footage of British bombs exploding over

Paris would be a propaganda own goal. It would not play well in the cinemas of still-neutral America. As it transpired, Hitler was keen to win over the French to his idea of a unified fascist Europe and so he vetoed the idea of a formal triumphal victory parade.

The Sonderzug Amerika

A second idea was to get at Hitler while he was travelling on his *Sonderzug* or special train, codenamed Amerika. But the carriages that housed the Führer and his entourage had been beefed up in 1939 with steel-plated panels and the train carried two platformed cars that housed its own anti-aircraft guns. The times when Hitler planned to use the train were known only to his closest SS aides and for secrecy it usually ran at night. A dummy train went ahead of the Amerika in case the tracks had been tampered with, or had a bomb placed under them, and all other trains were stopped or sidelined so that the Amerika could run at full speed between stations. It was a tough target to find and even tougher to hit.

We can get him at the Berghof

However, the tantalizing idea that Hitler was at his most accessible at the Berghof never went away. In June 1944 Major General Colin Gubbins, the director of the British Special Operations Executive (SOE), authorized a feasibility study for a sniper mission codenamed Operation Foxley. It owed much to the plot of the thriller by Geoffrey Household, who by this time had spent several years as a British spy in the Balkans and the Middle East. By this later stage in the war, British intelligence had gathered several thick dossiers concerning every aspect of the layout of the Berghof and its defences. The British had harvested this information from German prisoners of war who had visited or worked in some capacity at Hitler's mountain home. Much was known about Hitler's daily routines, especially his habit of walking through the woods to his preferred Teehaus.

Polish agents with a track record of success in 'black warfare' were considered for the job. Speaking excellent German and wearing SS uniforms, once through the wire perimeter they had a better chance than most of getting close enough to the target. They were also driven by an intense desire to avenge their devastated country and their mutilated nation. A British officer who was thought to be a crack shot, Captain Edmund Bennet, was also vaguely sounded out about the job. Although he was enjoying a glamorous posting as a military attaché in Washington, Bennet gallantly expressed interest in the mission, but he must have been privately relieved when Operation Foxley was quietly shelved.

The idea of decapitating the Reich certainly had its supporters in the War Office, as disposing of Hitler might have accelerated Germany's military collapse. Others, including the deputy head of the SOE's German section, Ronald Thornley, feared turning Hitler into a martyr and creating a future myth that Germany would have won the war if only he had survived. Ultimately the War Cabinet came around to the view that as the war had progressed Hitler had turned out to be the best general that the Allies could ever have. His continual interference in German military operations and his deep distrust of the men from Zossen had seriously hampered the German war effort, particularly his continued refusal to allow his generals to withdraw their men from untenable positions in order to rest and regroup. And in any case, what was the point of sending snipers to the Berghof on a suicide mission if no one knew if he was actually there?

The missing Führer

Hitler had seldom been seen in public since summer 1944, having never recovered his spirits after the sudden and almost complete annihilation of Army Group Centre by the Soviet Union's brilliant late summer offensive, Plan Bagration. In the greatest tactical triumph of the war, the Red Army destroyed 28 of AGC's 34 divisions in under eight weeks. Coupled with the progress being made in France and Italy by the Western Allies, Hitler knew that the war was effectively over. Allied intelligence believed that he was seriously ill and had in fact suffered from a suspected stroke. Dr Morell was keeping him going on a mixture of pills and injections, which included potent methamphetamines such as the 'combat drug' Pervitin. If using this stimulant brought him any temporary benefit, he was also afflicted by its well-known side-effects. He suffered from exhaustion and inertia for days and was unable to concentrate upon the war. It was known, however, that he had last been at his Rastenburg HQ in November 1944 and the Russians confirmed that the Wolf was no longer in his Lair when they occupied its damaged ruins in late January.

A dramatic last act?

By the beginning of 1945 Allied strategists suspected that Hitler was planning to make his last stand in the Obersalzberg at an 'Alpine Redoubt'. British 'Hitler specialists' also felt that this was very likely. It fitted in with what was known about his personal psychology and his interest in mythology and music. Hitler was known to be a lifelong admirer of Wagner's cataclysmic *Götterdammerung*, in which the fortress of Valhalla collapses around the gods in the last scenes. Allied planners speculated that he would choose a similarly glorious death in the mountains that spanned his two homelands of Austria and Bavaria. A number of intelligence reports suggested considerable construction and tunnelling activity in the hills around the Berghof.

In the last weeks of the war, Hitler's most loyal general, Sepp Dietrich, was known to have suddenly pulled his 6th Panzer Army and a number of well-equipped Waffen-SS units out of the Lake Balaton sector in Hungary. Dietrich had reached Vienna and it was assumed he was heading further west to join the Führer for the final defiant moments of the Third Reich. The thought of a bloody, protracted campaign in the Bavarian Alps was not welcomed by American and British commanders, especially those who had studied the exceptionally murderous Austro-Italian war that had been fought just a few miles away between 1915 and 1918.

As a precaution, on 25 April 1945 the RAF sent more than 300 bombers to the Obersalzberg in order to crush Hitler's potential Alamo. They did a good job of demolishing the visible buildings at the Berghof complex, though much of the underground network was relatively unscathed. Several British crewmen were killed on the mission, but their deaths were in vain. Hitler had already decided that he would fight to the bitter end and breathe his last in the centre of the Reich's capital city of Berlin. He had left the Berghof on 16 July 1944, and flown northwards, never to return.

20 July 1944
Stauffenberg

I n early April 1943, units of the 10th Panzer Division attached to Erwin
Rommel's Afrika Korps took up new defensive positions near Mezzouna.
This small central Tunisian town lay 45 miles (72 km) south-east of Sidi
Bouzid, the early Christian Roman town of Simingi. About another hour's drive
to the west was the hard, rocky landscape where the battle of the Kasserine
Pass had been played out five weeks before. The sides of the dry, stony roads
around Kasserine were still littered with the evidence of Rommel's recent
success. In a bitter five-day engagement in late February, the largely American
Allied battle group had lost almost 800 tanks and other vehicles and over 3,300
men killed and wounded. Another 3,000 Allied troops had gone missing in the
harsh Tunisian landscape. A combination of Rommel's cunning, his fondness
for battlefield tricks which had earned him the nickname Desert Fox and the
inexperience of the American troops and their commanders had resulted in a
short-term, tactical victory for the Afrika Korps. It had bought Rommel some
valuable time in which to reorganize his tired and depleting forces for the
desperate battles yet to come.

Strafed at Mezzouna

On 8 April a Curtiss P-40 Kittyhawk ground-attack fighter of the Royal
Australian Air Force spotted a German staff car hurtling along the dusty road
towards Mezzouna. It contained the operations officer of the 10th Panzers, who
was about to inspect the holding positions that some of its vehicles had taken
there. The Kittyhawk banked and came down on the car with its Browning
machine guns ablaze. The young lieutenant in the car was killed outright and

the senior officer, a lieutenant colonel, sustained numerous dreadful wounds from bullets and shrapnel throughout his body, but he survived the attack. He also survived the emergency surgery in the field hospital later that day, though he suffered permanent damage which amounted to the loss of an eye, two of his left-hand fingers and all of his right hand.

Back in Germany he was treated by the world-renowned surgeon Ernst Sauerbruch of Berlin's Charité Hospital, who was famed for his work on tuberculosis but was also an innovative expert in the field of prostheses for the war-wounded. Recuperating in a sanatorium near Munich, the officer received two 'gold' medals as compensation for his losses. More importantly, however, his injuries meant that his active service as a front-line officer in the war was over. At best, he could look forward to a dull desk job somewhere back in the Fatherland. Seeing out the war as a 'back-room boy' was not a pleasing prospect for Claus von Stauffenberg, a patriotic German and an effective soldier with a taste for action in the field.

A family of knights

Claus Philipp Maria Schenk Graf von Stauffenberg was born in 1907 in one of his family's four castles in Swabia in southern Germany. The counts of Stauffenberg traced their ancestry back to an Imperial Knight in 1251 and they were especially proud of their additional hereditary title of Schenk or Cup-bearer. It denoted their centuries of service and close connections to the royal Hohenzollern family. As a boy, Claus was clearly highly intelligent, sensitive and exceptionally well read. When he was a young man, he and his brothers developed a lasting interest in the various 'circles' of writers, poets and philosophers who were seeking to nurture a new, more moral German society throughout the 1920s and 1930s. Nevertheless, in 1926, at the age of 19, he joined the Weimar Republic military organization, the Reichswehr, as a cadet officer in his family cavalry regiment and later attended the Kriegsakademie in Berlin. Although he received a thorough education in modern technological warfare there, he retained a lifelong interest in horses and argued for their continuing value in military logistics. They were certainly useful when the panzers and trucks froze up in Russia in winter 1941.

A model soldier

Stauffenberg's first 'active' service was as part of a column that entered the Sudetenland after Britain and France abandoned Czechoslovakia to its fate in

Claus von Stauffenberg was the driving force behind the July 1944 plot to assassinate Hitler.

September 1938. He participated in the Polish Blitzkrieg the following year and for his service in the Fall of France in 1940 he was awarded the Iron Cross First Class. By the time of Operation Barbarossa in June 1941 Stauffenberg was attached to the Wehrmacht's High Command on the Eastern Front. On 8 November 1942 the Western Allies launched Operation Torch and over the next eight days an impressive Anglo-American battle group landed in Morocco and Algeria. The 10th Panzer Division was diverted first to Vichy France and then to French North Africa to meet that threat, which led to Stauffenberg's life-changing incident on the road to Mezzouna. Despite his various disabilities, there had to be a useful, valuable role in the Wehrmacht for an able man of his intelligence and experience. When he was discharged from hospital in July 1943, however, he found that he had been re-designated as a staff officer in the Reserve Army in Berlin, where he could expect to shuffle paper at his desk until the end of hostilities.

The replacement army

In the peaceful Weimar years, new recruits to the Reichswehr normally learned their new 'trade' of soldiering with their own regiments at their home bases in Germany. But with almost all units now away on active service, the initial training of new soldiers was undertaken by the *Ersatzheer*, or replacement army. In September 1943, Stauffenberg was assigned to the *Erstazheer*'s HQ in an office block at Bendlerstrasse in Berlin. One of his superior officers there, General Friedrich Olbricht, was a vocal critic of Hitler and was correctly presumed by many to be an active oppositionist. Through Olbricht, Stauffenberg crossed paths again with Henning von Tresckow: they had briefly met in Russia. He also met Axel von dem Bussche, who would attempt to assassinate Hitler at the exhibition of winter uniforms later that year. Stauffenberg was gradually being surrounded by oppositionist comrades and his own long, slow transformation from loyal officer into a leader of anti-Hitler resistance was well under way.

A difficult decision

Many German 'resisters of conscience', such as the White Rose students or the anti-Nazi pastor Dietrich Bonhöffer, instantly and instinctively understood the inherent evil of Nazism from the outset. Like many 'military resisters' of his class, however, Stauffenberg held deeply conflicted views about Hitler and his movement. He agreed with and admired many aspects of Nazi ideology and like millions of Germans of the period he recognized Hitler's strengths as a leader and conveniently overlooked his failings. In his youth, Stauffenberg shared the everyday prejudiced assumptions about Jews that had traditionally informed 'Aryan' Germans of every social class and he later admitted to making the casual anti-Semitic remarks that especially peppered the conversation of Germans of his rank. He was also a conservative nationalist and therefore implacably opposed to the dictates of the Versailles Settlement. Even in 1944, when the war was clearly lost, he took the view that Germany should only agree to a new armistice and peace settlement if the Allies guaranteed to restore the eastern border as it had stood in 1914.

He went further, believing that lands and cities further east that had once been held by the Order of the Teutonic Knights, such as the Hansa city of Reval, should be reincorporated within the Fatherland. And he shared the assumptions of his class about the non-German peoples of central and eastern Europe, implicitly accepting many aspects of National Socialist racial policy. Like many Germans at the time, he unthinkingly viewed the Slavs as self-evidently inferior to Germans, in the same way that many Britons of the period considered certain peoples of their Empire to be 'less developed'.

Stauffenberg also admired the Nazi vision of a disciplined society, a nation of comrades, that respected its local communities and local traditions and stood against the corroding spirit of modern life generated in the ever-larger urban centres. In theory at least, Adolf Hitler and his movement seemed to place a greater emphasis on a moral approach to life that valued family, community and loyalty. Nazism promised to be an antidote to the commercialism and corruption that Stauffenberg and others of his class felt had seeped into German life as a result of capitalism and industrialization. And like all men of the Wehrmacht, in 1934 he had taken the sacred oath of loyalty to the Führer. Breaking that oath was going to be a difficult decision for a man of Stauffenberg's breeding and beliefs.

No Nazi

Though Stauffenberg appreciated some key aspects of Hitler's programme, he never joined the NSDAP and when questioned by Tresckow and others about his politics he made it very clear that he had no plans to do so. Despite their appeals to German history and tradition, he distrusted the Nazis' modern approach to politics, which often depended on a 'gangsterist' willingness to resort to illegality and 'the politics of the cosh and the gun'. In many regards, he was a man of another, more distant era. Growing up as a Stauffenberg he experienced a boyhood and adolescence in which he shifted from one castle or manor house to another and he could hardly be unaware of his family's long history and its traditions of service to the community and the nation. He was a practising Catholic throughout his life, probably because he understood the ways in which his historic church helped to bind German society together, rather than because of any burning faith. And he took great intellectual pleasure from the German Romantic 'medievalist' poems and paintings of the 19th century, which had done much to promote a proud German nationalism.

From all these ingredients in his life, he had distilled a personal chivalric code that was further informed by his reading of current moral philosophers and poets such as Stefan Georg. Initially he genuinely believed that Adolf Hitler was a man of some principle and, until Stalingrad, that he was a highly competent military strategist. The costly Russian fiasco dispelled that illusion and a conversation with Axel von dem Bussche shattered the other. A shocked Stauffenberg listened as von dem Bussche related his chilling experience at the western Ukrainian city of Dubno on 24 October 1942. He had stumbled upon an SS *Einsatzgruppe* busily exterminating the town's Jewish population and the things he saw that day compelled him to join the resistance to Hitler. His words had exactly the same effect on Stauffenberg.

A natural leader

Claus von Stauffenberg had many advantages in life, not least of which was his personal demeanour and appearance. He was charming, good-humoured and handsome, even once he had acquired the patch over his missing left eye. Fit and athletic and 6ft 3in (191 cm) tall, he cut an imposing figure. He was also a tireless, dynamic man with the energy to undertake all the unseen background chores that were a necessary part of effectively planning any project, let alone one that involved assassinating a heavily guarded head of state. In addition, he was used to commanding others, so he understood the personal qualities needed to inspire people to participate in missions that might lead them straight to the underground torture chambers at Number 8, Prinz-Albrecht-Strasse in Berlin, headquarters of the Gestapo.

During the winter of 1943–44 the unofficial leadership of the resistance cadre in the Wehrmacht devolved upon Stauffenberg's shoulders, in large part because its other leaders were no longer available. Henning von Tresckow was posted to the Eastern Front in October 1943 and within weeks had been appointed Chief of Staff of the 2nd Army. As a commander in the field, he was heavily restricted in his movements and required permission from Berlin to take leave from his post, even if undertaking official business. Moreover, although his post was senior, it gave him no automatic right of access to the Führer, so he was effectively marooned at the Front and could play no further part in resistance plots. Hans Oster had been dismissed from his Abwehr post in late 1943, when his involvement in helping Jews escape from Germany was discovered. He had also been warned by friends that he was now under constant Gestapo surveillance, so he too took no further part in resistance work.

In early 1944, Himmler finally convinced Hitler that the Abwehr, or German intelligence, was a nest of vipers, many of whom had long been actively plotting against the government. He could also prove that Abwehr agents had been responsible for saving hundreds of Jews from the Gestapo, which probably angered Hitler more. In February 1944 the Abwehr was abolished and all of its duties were now performed by an SS office supervised by Himmler. Several weeks later, the Abwehr's former leader, Admiral Canaris, was placed under house arrest.

Operation Valkyrie

If Stauffenberg was dismayed at the loss of these experienced comrades, he was delighted by one unexpected outcome of his paper-shuffling on Bendlerstrasse. Operation Valkyrie, a set of procedures drawn up and approved by the Führer in 1943, specified the actions to be carried out to counter a serious outbreak of public unrest in Germany. The Valkyrie plans identified all the military, security and communications facilities within the Reich and collated the contact details of each facility and its current commander. They also indicated how the contingents in these bases were to be deployed if they ever received the activation signal 'Valkyrie' from Berlin. In circumstances where the Army High Command office in Berlin was temporarily unable to respond to the unrest or to communicate effectively, the Valkyrie plan ordered the *Ersatzheer* commanders in their secure offices at the Bendlerblock to take control of the situation. The initial plan had been drawn up to allay Nazi fears of an uprising by the millions of foreign slave labourers who had been pressed into the German industrial economy. As they were thought to be over ten million in number, they represented a serious threat to the stability of the Reich.

In the deteriorating atmosphere of early 1944, however, it was also thought that the Valkyrie precautions might be useful if the enemy attempted a parachute assault on the capital, or even if a putsch was attempted by rogue elements within the State. One of Stauffenberg's duties was to maintain the plan documents and amend them as circumstances required, and over time Stauffenberg and his allies within the Reserve Army did amend them, turning them into a tool that could be used to bring about a swift *coup d'état*. In effect Stauffenberg created a parallel Operation Valkyrie that would supersede the original in an emergency. The first thing needed to trigger the coup was a successful hit on Hitler. The second requirement was a plausible interim government that could be in place and ready to act instantly, while others such as Himmler and Göring were still numbed by events. Several army officers were willing to support a shadow government, but the most senior generals such as Field Marshal Erich von Manstein were not minded to commit mutiny. Significantly, however, they did not give the plotters away either. Stauffenberg decided to plough on, believing that once Hitler had been eliminated, new leaders would inevitably emerge from the Wehrmacht's senior ranks.

Meeting up with the Führer

Managing to realize the first requirement of the plot suddenly became much more feasible on 20 June 1944. Stauffenberg learned that he had been promoted to colonel and appointed Chief of Staff to the Commander-in-Chief of the Reserve Army, General Friedrich Fromm. In this new post, it was Stauffenberg's duty to compile and update information on army recruiting numbers and the readiness of new recruits for front-line duties. Given the importance of this data for Hitler and his senior planners, Stauffenberg was also required to deliver his reports to the Führer in person and to do so regularly. There was now a strong possibility that the first requirement for a successful parallel Valkyrie operation could be met. A bomb could be smuggled into Hitler's presence whether he was at Rastenburg, the Berghof or the Reich Chancellery. The only problem was that Stauffenberg would have to do the bloody job himself.

Three trips to the Alps

Between 7 June and 11 July Stauffenberg met Hitler three times at the Berghof. At the first meeting, there were only documents in his case. His aim was to get to know the layout of the Berghof and make a favourable impression on Hitler and his courtiers. He was met with a warm welcome by the Führer, who had been told of his admirable performance both in the field and as a desk-bound staff officer. On 6 July he did have explosives in his case, but they were not destined for Hitler. Stauffenberg had taken them along to pass on to General

Hellmuth Stieff, an indecisive oppositionist. The general had previously raised the possibility of exploding a bomb when Hitler visited Schloss Klessheim, the magnificent baroque palace just outside Salzburg, but in the event he was not disposed to take the idea any further. So Stauffenberg went back to Berlin with a full briefcase. By the time he returned to the Berghof five days later he realized that he could no longer wait for someone else to kill Hitler. The job had to be done quickly and he was probably the best man to do it, even though he would be the second victim of his own bomb.

And Himmler too!

As he flew south to Bavaria yet again on 11 July, any self-pity that he felt was soon dispelled by the information that Himmler was also expected at the Berghof. Killing both bastards with one bomb was an unexpected bonus and it made excellent tactical sense. Himmler was an intelligent and ruthless commander and was the most likely successor to a dead Hitler. With his fanatical Waffen-SS legions under his full command, the war might very well drag on for many additional months and like Hitler he would never surrender. His responsibility for Nazi war crimes across Europe meant that death on an Allied gallows was his probable fate, although he carried his own private supply of prussic acid in order to cheat the hangman. As long as he breathed, however, Himmler would continue to take thousands of good men with him to the grave. In the event, Stauffenberg did not get his bonus as Himmler was detained elsewhere, but the idea was a good one and so he decided to postpone the explosion until his next trip to the Obersalzberg. Hitler was spared for the moment.

Dry run at Wolfsschanze

Four days later Stauffenberg was hurriedly summoned to a day of conferences at the Rastenburg complex. By now the British SOE plastic explosive that he carried in his briefcase had racked up some mileage: it was the same Abwehr stock that had not been detonated in the frozen brandy bomb more than 15 months earlier. Stauffenberg had no difficulty carrying his briefcase around Wolf's Lair and could have set it off at any one of the three meetings that day which both he and Hitler attended. The reasons for his decision to postpone exploding the bomb therefore remain a source of dispute.

Thanks to his new post, he was now in Hitler's presence on a regular basis, so he may have wanted to wait until a later meeting where he had the chance to get at other senior Party figures as well as the Führer. Or perhaps he might

have struggled to activate the device in the limited time available to him, being unfamiliar with the method of detonation and having only three damaged fingers to work with. He first had to make sure that Hitler was actually in the target room. Then he had to find a reason to leave so he could set the bomb. Finally, he had to return and place his case in the optimal location. If he was to avoid Hitler's fate he would have to excuse himself from the room again. Not only did he need to control the inevitable signs of stress under pressure, but he also had to hope that the Leibstandarte SS guards saw nothing unusual in his behaviour.

20 July 1944: detonation difficulties

Five days later Stauffenberg was back in East Prussia and determined to detonate, come what may. There were clear signs back in Berlin that Himmler's new SS officials, who were now responsible for military intelligence and security, took their job much more seriously than Admiral Canaris and Oster had done. Several oppositionist officers had been arrested and were now guests of special interest at Prinz-Albrecht-Strasse. No matter how brave they were, it was only a matter of time before they cracked and the entire resistance 'network' imploded.

This time, Stauffenberg had no choice but to carry his plan through. For the fourth time in just over three weeks he was in a room with Hitler, carrying a bomb and risking exposure as a traitor and certain death. And still there were unexpected complications in his way. The time of the planned meeting with Hitler was suddenly changed. It was brought forward so that Hitler would be able to discuss several pressing matters with Mussolini in more detail in the afternoon. This left far less time than expected for Stauffenberg and his adjutant, Oberleutnant Werner von Heaften, to assemble and set the bomb.

Under the pretext of Stauffenberg needing to change into a fresh shirt, they used the quarters of a fellow officer who was stationed at the complex. They were halfway through the job when they were interrupted by an aide at the door, reminding them that the meeting with the Führer was about to start in five minutes. Stauffenberg and Heaften managed to conceal the bomb from the aide but lost more precious seconds. As a result, Stauffenberg carried only one primed slab of explosive into the conference room. There was no time to set the fuse of the second slab. And under immense pressure neither Stauffenberg nor his aide thought to place the 'spare' plastic explosive in his briefcase, which would have added something extra to the blast. Due to yet another last-minute change to Hitler's timetable, the bomb that Stauffenberg placed under the table, barely a metre from its target, was seriously underpowered.

Mission accomplished?

The conference room was in a long, low building which consisted of a reinforced concrete roof sitting on a row of square brick columns. At 10 m (33 ft) long and around 4 m (13 ft) wide, the room comfortably held a group of between 20 and 25 participants. In the centre was a heavy oak table covered in maps, papers, notebooks and pencils. It was not a pleasant room, but several windows offered views of the mature woods that helped to shield the complex from Soviet spotter planes. Stauffenberg was late and a briefing on news from the East was already under way. Stauffenberg had informed Hitler's aides that his hearing had still not recovered from his Tunisian 'incident' so an empty seat close to the Führer had been left for him as requested. Hitler was sitting only two seats away on Stauffenberg's left. Stauffenberg placed his briefcase on the ground and then, 'remembering' that he had to make a phone call, he left the room. There was nothing unusual in this. Hitler's briefing conferences were not solemn nor static occasions. In addition to the gathered Wehrmacht officers questioning and conferring with the current briefing officer, there were adjutants bringing new messages or necessary documents and maps and secretaries and stenographers hammering on their keys. Stauffenberg's disappearance was barely noticed.

Carnage and confusion

At 12.42 p.m. a number of staff employed at Wolf's Lair heard an explosion and ignored it. The anti-aircraft teams were either testing their guns, they thought, or animals had wandered into the minefields that ringed the complex perimeter. In the conference block, however, all was carnage and confusion. Wooden roof beams had collapsed into the room and acrid smoke from the explosion and from burning maps and documents mixed with the dust of what had been the plaster ceiling lingered in the air. The central oak table was now a thousand shards and splinters and the windows and doors of the room had been blown out by the blast.

Ten of the participants at the meeting were very badly injured and eventually four would die. They included Colonel Brandt, who should have been killed by the brandy bomb. The first to die was Hitler's civilian stenographer Heinrich Berger, who lost both legs and simply bled away on the floor. Ironically, the bomb's real target was among the lightly injured. Hitler sustained only relatively minor cuts, burns and bruises. A very large number of small fragments of the oak table had done some superficial damage to his legs but they were easily removed. At first stunned and outraged, within an hour the Führer was already joking with his aides, secretaries and his valet and reminding all who would listen of his miraculous invincibility. That afternoon he entertained Mussolini by showing him his badly tattered clothing.

Calm in the capital

Within two hours Stauffenberg was back in Berlin, looking to initiate the second phase of the plot. He imagined that Hitler was dead and the revised version of Operation Valkyrie was now in full swing. However, he knew the coup was not going to plan as soon as he arrived at the airport. His driver had already deserted him by not turning up and he had to make his own way to the HQ on Bendlerstrasse. On arrival, he found far fewer conspirators there than expected and those who were at their posts were paralysed by uncertainty and fear. The orders to instigate Operation Valkyrie had gone out from the Bendlerblock to regional command centres but nervous officers in most of them decided to wait and hedge their bets. There had been no communication from Hitler's HQ as the SS had quickly imposed an effective communications blackout. Very soon, however, the airwaves were full of messages confirming that the Führer was well and that a plot by traitors in the Reserve Army had been foiled. Regional commanders should only trust orders from Reichsführer SS Himmler, who was in full command of the situation.

Stauffenberg did what he could to lift the spirits of those who stayed with him, phoning senior men who were needed for the resistance. Some troops did obey the fake Valkyrie orders and Goebbels' Ministry building was temporarily surrounded. By early evening it was clear that the regime was holding fast. Major Otto Remer, commanding officer of the Greater Germany Guards Battalion, had taken his men out on to the streets of Berlin as ordered by 'Valkyrie', initially believing that Himmler and Goebbels had launched a purge against Hitler loyalists. After a brief telephone conversation with the Führer, however, Remer's men closed down the government quarter and the coup in Berlin fizzled out. By eight o'clock the few remaining insurgents were besieged in the Bendlerblock by SS units. A struggle inside the building broke out between the oppositionists and other 'loyalist' officers of the Reserve Army, who had been unaware of the plot, and in the ensuing gunfight Stauffenberg was badly injured in the shoulder.

The diminutive Major General Helmuth Stieff is taken away by police after the attempt on Hitler's life in July 1944.

By midnight, the head of the Reserve Army had tidied up the mess. General Fromm had known of the plot and was sympathetic to it, but he had not participated in it. Earlier in that confusing and desperate day he had been locked in his office by conspirators who had distrusted him. Fromm was badly compromised by the day's events but decided that there might be a way to save his skin. Hitler had already ordered that Stauffenberg and his comrades should not be summarily executed because he wanted to deal with the traitors in his own time and in his own way. But Fromm hoped to demonstrate his loyalty by pretending not to have received the order in all the confusion. By shooting the traitors right away, he could display his fury with those who had attempted to murder his beloved leader. Around midnight, Stauffenberg and his aide von Heaften, plus the oppositionists General Olbricht and his aide Quernheim, were dragged out into the Bendlerblock courtyard. There they were shot without trial or ceremony by a ten-man firing squad supplied by Major Remer. The faithful adjutant von Heaften flung himself forward and took some of the bullets intended for his senior officer. The chivalrous Stauffenberg is said to have called on God to save Holy Germany.

Women Against Hitler

E lise Hampel learned that her brother was dead in late summer 1940. A soldier in the Wehrmacht, he had been killed in action in the Western campaign some weeks before. She knew who was to blame for her brother's death. Elise was a woman of limited education as her formal schooling had ended when she left elementary school to work as a maid. Yet in her grief and despair she scribbled her thoughts down on the notification that had come in the post that morning – Hitler, madman, warmonger. These first few words gave her an idea of how she could fight back against the Nazi regime. With the help of her husband Otto she would write messages expressing her hatred of Hitler and his war, to encourage her fellow Berliners to rise up and rebel. She would write her thoughts on postcards: 'Wake up German people, we must free ourselves from Hitler. There is no freedom under this devilish government.' Elise and Otto posted some of the cards while others were left in tenement stairwells or on shop windowsills; anywhere that someone might see them, pick them up and read them. Over the next two years they left more than 200 of these message cards in various places in Berlin. It was the only way that Elise could demonstrate her opposition to Hitlerism.

Powerless to resist

Elise and Otto were typical of millions of powerless Germans in the Third Reich. It's likely that the Hampels never voted for the NSDAP back in the Weimar days. They lived in the largely working-class district of Wedding in north-west Berlin, where most people voted Social Democrat or Communist before 1933. Like millions of Germans they were caught unawares by the speed and thoroughness with which the Nazis transformed the democratic republic into a totalitarian dictatorship. Even if they had dreamed of killing Hitler, working-class Germans like the Hampels had no access to the weapons, explosives, contacts and resources needed for the most basic plot. Their only way of expressing their opposition to the regime was to try and make their thoughts and feelings known to others by writing them down in simple phrases.

Hunting for the postcard terrorists

The Gestapo were infuriated by 'the postcard terrorists'. A steady stream of cards with anti-Nazi messages inscribed in black ink was handed in to the police by frightened Berliners, worried that the Gestapo had left the cards for them to find and report as a test of their loyalty. Slowly and methodically the Gestapo mapped the appearance of the cards and narrowed down the probable location of the perpetrators. Postboxes were monitored and local shopkeepers were reminded to provide any information about customers who purchased blank postcards in any quantity. Eventually, in autumn 1942, Elise and Otto were detected and arrested. Their act of rebellion had been personal and feeble but in the eyes of the Nazi state it was treason.

A heroic teacher

Throughout the Nazi period, a picture of the Great Leader adorned the walls of every classroom in Germany. Textbooks and wall maps, especially in the key subject of history, reflected the National Socialist world-view. Thus Weimar period classroom wall maps showing the origins of human civilization along the Nile and the great rivers of Asia were all destroyed. They were replaced by maps that clearly showed that the dawn of mankind and its first great cultural achievements all took place in the Germanic heartland between the Rhine and the Elbe. Similarly, Weimar wall maps of Europe contained tables that gave the distance in kilometres between the great cities of Europe. These were taken down after 1933 and replaced by the new approved maps, which measured the distance between the likes of London and Berlin in terms of the estimated flight times of enemy bombers reaching the German capital in a future war. None of these educational innovations were implemented at the school run by Elisabeth von Thadden, first near Heidelberg in the 1920s and 1930s and then at the safer location of Tutzing in Bavaria in 1940.

Elisabeth was a wealthy and well-educated woman from a deeply Protestant background. Her boarding school was established with the specific aim of encouraging girls to be independent, modern young women whose morals were grounded on Christian values and ethics. She had read and admired the writings of the educationalist Kurt Hahn and after 1933 she continued to follow the precepts of similar progressive thinkers, rather than the regulations of the National Socialist Ministry for Schools. And she continued to enrol Jewish girls for several years after the Nazi revolution. As her first school was in a country house in a relatively secluded location, it took time for her activities to come to the full attention of the Nazi authorities.

After the move to Tutzing, however, she was soon denounced by a fervent Nazi pupil. The lack of Nazi educational paraphernalia and the emphasis upon readings from the Jewish Old Testament in the school's daily worship were enough for the Bavarian state authorities to 'nationalize' or confiscate the school. After Thadden was expelled from its governing board she moved to Berlin, where she served as a Red Cross nursing assistant, but she inevitably drifted into the company of like-minded fellows; that is, those with anti-Nazi political and philosophical beliefs. She remained on the Gestapo's list of marked men and women and was eventually scooped up by them in early 1944, while she was working as a nurse in occupied France.

Acts of kindness, friendship and faith

Many other German women resisted the Nazi government in similar 'small' ways. Their opposition often began as an expression of human decency rather than a political act. The half-Dutch Cato van Beck was horrified by the treatment of a family of Jewish neighbours who were being deported 'elsewhere'. Cato first reacted to the harshness of the Nazis by giving food to French prisoners of war. She then graduated to distributing leaflets pleading for peace and calling on German men to resist conscription into the armed forces. She quickly disappeared into a Gestapo prison.

In the Weimar days, Johanna Kirchner had been a Social Democratic Party (SPD) activist. When Hitler assumed power in 1933 and the party was declared illegal she moved to the Saarland, which was then still administered by the League of Nations. Once the Saar rejoined Germany in 1935, she moved on to France. She then helped former colleagues and friends in the SPD to make their way out of the Reich. In 1942 she was arrested by the security police of Vichy France and handed over to the Gestapo.

Eva-Maria Buch met the journalist Wilhelm Guddorf while working in a bookshop and he introduced her to the Red Orchestra, a loose organization of dissenters and plotters that never existed in a formal way but was still a thorn in the Nazis' side. During a series of Gestapo raids on the Red Orchestra Guddorf attempted to hide her, but she was arrested on 11 October 1942. Buch was then accused of translating an article meant for slave labourers into French.

Helene Gotthold was a Jehovah's Witness. Her church was distrusted and despised by the Nazi authorities for its pacifism and its staunch loyalty to God and to no other authority. Witnesses refused to swear loyalty to Hitler, use the Hitler salute or serve in the German military forces. As a result, over 10,000 Jehovah's Witnesses ended up in Nazi camps, where they were exceptionally badly treated. Gotthold had been arrested for her faith in 1937 and had miscarried as a result of Gestapo beatings but in February 1944 she was back in a Nazi prison, alongside her husband. Her crimes this time were helping conscientious objectors to hide from the police and holding Jehovah's Witness meetings, which were specifically forbidden in the Third Reich.

Two views of paradise

In the summer of 1942, Joseph Goebbels' Propaganda Ministry held a major exhibition in the Lustgarten, the formal park on Museum Island in central Berlin that Hitler had paved over and turned into a space for political rallies and military parades. The exhibition carried the ironic title: 'The Soviet Paradise.' Squads of Nazi journalists, photographers and cameramen had been sent into occupied western Russia as the Wehrmacht pushed east. Their mission was to collect evidence of the poverty, squalor and misery of daily life in the USSR, under the rule of its Jewish–Bolshevik masters. The exhibition was a great success and was seen by more than 1.3 million visitors, most of whom went home glad to be living in a German rather than a Russian totalitarian state.

Not far away, however, on Kurfürstendamm, a small group of protestors chose to disagree. On 17 May 1942 they distributed posters bearing the legend: 'The Nazi Paradise – War, Hunger, Lies, Gestapo. How much longer?' One of the protestors was the 18-year-old Liane Berkowitz. She was tracked down by the Gestapo and arrested in September that year, charged with being a member of the Red Orchestra. By this stage in the war there were several disparate groups and many individuals in Germany who felt moved to openly criticize the Nazi regime. They were barely connected with each other, but it suited Goebbels and the Gestapo to sweep them all under one banner, which suggested that they were all communists and were acting in a concerted way.

Communist opposition and espionage

There was some truth in the Nazi claim that oppositionists in Germany were Soviet agents. The Communist Party of Germany (KPD) had been quickly squashed in 1933 along with all other political parties, but Moscow still had its supporters and agents within the Reich. Some of these were women and several of them went beyond acts of dissent to commit espionage and treason. As early as 1935, Liselotte Herrmann had been exposed as a Soviet agent. A communist from her schooldays, in the mid-1930s she worked as a secretary and typist at her family's engineering works. There she had access to contracts and documents that revealed the massive expansion of the underground armaments store at Celle near Hanover and the development of the Dornier Aircraft Company at Friedrichshafen on Lake Constance. Copies of these were forwarded to communist agents in Switzerland and France until Liselotte's activities were discovered by the Gestapo.

During the war, several German women with a communist background took their opposition activities to a higher level. Ursula Goetze, a former Young Communist, began her career in the resistance by organizing and distributing food and clothes to Jewish families and to the wives and children of imprisoned anti-Nazis during the 1930s. Shortly before the start of the Second World War she went to London to visit some Jewish friends, but in August 1939 she left the relative safety of England to return to Germany. She believed it was her duty to resist the war that Hitler was clearly planning. Her flat in Berlin became a base for listening to foreign broadcasts, for conveying oppositionist information and for meeting contacts. Ursula also took part in the Nazi Paradise protest in 1942, as did Hilde Coppi, a former KPD member whose flat was another important 'listening station' for news and messages from Radio Moscow.

Ernestine Diwisch was one of several German women involved in an organization called the Soldiers' Council, which operated in German Austria during the war. In her teenage years, Diwisch had been a member of the Red Falcons, a youth communist group, and she remained loyal to the KPÖ or Austrian Communist Party. In 1942 she was a worker in an aircraft factory at Wiener Neustadt south of Vienna, but she remained a political activist. The Soldiers' Council produced pamphlets and a small newspaper that tried to encourage men in the Wehrmacht to desert and make links with communist groups. This led to her arrest in May 1943, when she was charged with high treason and 'supporting the enemy'.

Female spies

A number of German women undertook activities that were clearly espionage. Käte Niederkirchner was expelled from Germany in 1933 for being a communist and a trades union organizer. She then moved to the Soviet Union. In the first two years of the war she worked on German-language broadcasts for Radio Moscow and was involved in the interrogation and 're-education' of German prisoners of war. However, determined to do even more to stop the Nazis, in October 1943 she was parachuted into Poland, carrying information for the resistance movement in Germany. Unfortunately, en route to Berlin she fell into the hands of the SS and found herself in Ravensbrück concentration camp.

Libertas Schulze-Boysen and Elisabeth Schumacher were both arrested for recording information about Nazi war crimes committed against the Jews, enemy POWs and the civilian populations in occupied territories. Both had met Soviet agents and passed on information as part of their mission and Schumacher was one of several female oppositionists who tried to inform the Soviets about Operation Barbarossa.

Ilse Stöbe, a converted former Nazi, and the German-American Mildred Harnack were both arrested for contacting Soviet agents with the same aim of warning Moscow of Hitler's intentions in the East. Although innocent of any crime, Stöbe's mother was also arrested at the same time. She ended her days in Ravensbrück.

The Solf Circle

On 10 September 1943, the progressive educationalist Elisabeth von Thadden, who featured earlier in this chapter, held a small party for friends at her flat in Berlin. Most of the guests were connected in one way or another with the elegant 55-year-old lady who seemed to be at the centre of all the chat that evening. She was Johanna Solf, widow of a distinguished diplomat of the Imperial and Weimar days. Since 1936 she and her daughter Lagi, Countess von Ballestrem, had held occasional meetings with like-minded friends to discuss 'the Hitler problem' and the perilous implications of his policies. Over time, they used their influence and contacts to hide Jewish friends and provide them with the money and documents needed to escape the Reich. By 1943, the circle around the Solf women was also discussing the future of Germany after its inevitable defeat, with another group of upper-class dissidents. They had gathered around Helmuth Graf von Moltke, a landowner, distinguished jurist and bearer of one of the most revered names in German history. Moltke's group of anti-Nazis met far from prying eyes at his Kreisau estate in Prussian Silesia.

Dr Reckzeh

One of the guests that evening was a new face to the group, a young Swiss assistant doctor working at the Charité hospital under the renowned surgeon Professor Sauerbruch. He was charming, handsome, a relaxed conversationalist and he instantly meshed with the other guests. They were the usual mixture to be found at a meeting at this social level: diplomats, intellectuals and senior businessmen. In the course of the evening, the young man, Paul Reckzeh, made several remarks about Hitler and the progress of the war. His comments were as critical as was possible in a social situation in wartime Berlin, but they encouraged others in the flat to confide in the young foreigner. They asked him if he would convey some letters to their friends in Switzerland and Reckzeh was only too happy to oblige. Their letters and his report were soon sitting on Heinrich Himmler's desk.

Dr Reckzeh, aka Agent Robby, was rewarded with a promotion to the rank of staff surgeon in the Nazi Todt Organization, which was responsible for the millions of foreign slave labourers in Germany's mines and factories. Himmler now had all the information he needed to sweep up a group of plotters and defeatists that had been irritating both him and the Führer for some time. Seventy-four suspects connected to the Solfs were eventually rounded up. Johanna and Lagi fled to Austria but were captured by the Gestapo and detained in Ravensbrück. However, a fortunate Allied bombing raid in February 1945 destroyed all the files held on them and also killed Hitler's 'Hanging Judge', Roland Freisler. A second trial was arranged in late April but they were saved again by the chaos of those final days of the Reich and the arrival of the Red Army in Berlin.

The price of resistance

Both Johanna and her daughter survived the war, although Lagi never recovered from the torture she experienced in Gestapo hands and died relatively young in 1955. The other 16 female oppositionists mentioned in this chapter were executed. Fourteen of them were beheaded by guillotine in the House of Death within Plötzensee Prison. The Austrian Ernestine Diwisch was guillotined in Vienna by an apparatus that had been constructed there after the Nazi takeover. Pleas for clemency were made for the three younger women in the group;

18-year-old Liane Berkowitz and Eva-Maria Buch and Cato van Beck, both 22 years old. These appeals made by their families were all dismissed by Hitler, although the execution of the pregnant Hilde Coppi was delayed for several months to allow her to give birth and nurse her child.

Two of the women, Johanna Kirchner and Mildred Harnack, were initially sentenced to long terms in prison. In Kirchner's case, Judge Roland Freisler reviewed the case and felt that the original sentence of ten years' hard labour had been far too lenient. This time she was sentenced to death. Hitler personally intervened in the German-American Harnack's situation. He was annoyed by the international attention that her case had attracted and by the many pleas for clemency made on her behalf. Her original prison sentence was overturned and she was beheaded in February 1943, the only American woman to be executed by personal order of the Führer.

Käte Niederkirchner was clearly a Soviet spy. She had no trial and was simply shot out of hand at Ravensbrück concentration camp. Otto Hampel went to the guillotine in the same batch of victims as his wife Elise.

CHAPTER 20

July 1944–April 1945
Aftermath and Retribution

In the weeks and months after the bombing at Rastenburg, a proud Führer made many references to the unique protection that he received from 'divine Providence'. He had survived four long years in the trenches, multiple attacks from communists, Jews, Christians and lunatics plus continual conspiracies within an army that was poisoned against him. Surviving the Stauffenberg attack was a special moment for celebration and retribution. But Hitler was nothing if not generous. He ordered the production of a unique Führer Wounds Badge, to be awarded to those who had shared that special moment in his destiny in the bomb-blasted conference room. It came in gold, silver and black variants to reflect the fact that some of the recipients were dead while others had suffered wounds of varying severity. Each badge was accompanied by an elaborate formal certificate, personally signed by the exultant Hitler.

Punishing the Wehrmacht

It was now time to punish the army for its deep involvement in what Goebbels described as 'their historic moment of shame'. Every soldier in the Wehrmacht had to do penance for the crimes of the oppositionist conspirators. The entire army was made to re-swear its oath of personal loyalty to the Führer and its traditional form of salute was abolished. Instead, all troops were now required to adopt the German or Hitler greeting, uttered with right hand outstretched. Failure to adhere to this directive would be taken as a sign of latent treachery. Many *Kameraden* at the Front later recounted how their officers read out the order to them and then casually signed off in the normal Wehrmacht way. They also remembered that it was always wise to obey the salute ruling when SS personnel were about.

Blood guilt

The Wolf's Lair outrage was a marvellous opportunity for a thorough purge of the treacherous elements within the army. Hitler and Himmler were soon deep in conversation as to how best to eradicate that Zossen spirit once and for all. The SS and Gestapo nets would be cast wide and those that ended up in them would include active resisters, those who knew about resistance activities and committed treason by remaining silent and, at Himmler's insistence, the families and relatives of the offenders.

During the later years of the Third Reich, the Nazi legal system made increasing use of the legal concept of *Sippenhaft* or blood guilt. It was believed that in ancient Teutonic times the entire clan of a guilty offender was liable to contribute to the *Wergeld*, or compensation, that was due to his victim. Himmler simplified the concept to mean that the families and children of arrested conspirators shared in their guilt by association. They must have known what was going on and therefore chose not to inform the authorities. Stern measures were needed to deter future conspirators, Himmler argued, and men undergoing interrogation would be more pliable and co-operative if they knew that their loved ones were in the clutches of the SS.

Punishing the Stauffenbergs

Himmler vowed to erase the name of Stauffenberg from German history so the entire family was arrested, regardless of age or guilt. Claus's pregnant wife Elisabeth, known as 'Nina', was sent to Ravensbrück while her children were confiscated and held in a distant orphanage under new names. Even elderly and quite distant members of the Stauffenberg clan found themselves behind Gestapo bars. Claus's brother Berthold was already doomed as he was deeply implicated in the 20 July plot. On 10 August he was condemned in the *Volksgerichtshof* or People's Court to death by hanging. His executioner was the sadistic hangman Wilhelm Röttger, who favoured the traditional 'Austrian short drop' which ensured that the victim endured a slow death by strangulation. Claus's other brother Alexander was a twice-wounded officer in the Wehrmacht, so it was clear that, stationed in Russia and then Greece, he had not been involved in the plot against Hitler. Nevertheless, he ended up in Dachau. His wife Melitta Schiller (or Melitta Schenk Gräfin von Stauffenberg) was also initially imprisoned in the camp system. She had particular reasons to fear Hitler and Himmler's desire to punish the Stauffenbergs. A patriotic German, Melitta was no supporter of the Nazi regime. She had made critical comments about Hitler in 1936 when her career as an aeronautical engineer came to a sudden end because of her racial origins. Her outstanding background in aero-mathematics and physics counted for less than her tainted blood: one of her grandfathers had been Jewish. It was only her unique skills and bravery as a test pilot that saved her from the fate of most other Germans of Jewish heritage. In fact, the importance of her wartime work was recognized by the Nazi authorities, who awarded her several decorations including the Iron Cross. Melitta's limited influence may have been enough to ensure that the 'imprisoned' Stauffenberg children were well treated and survived the war. Loyal to the Luftwaffe but never to Hitler, Melitta herself died in the last weeks of the war from injuries sustained when she was shot down by the US Air Force.

The People's Court

Many of the Wehrmacht officers implicated in the 20 July plot underwent the cynical ritual of a show trial at the People's Court in Berlin. Hitler's 'justice' was dispensed in a chamber that was dominated by a vast swastika drape and an outsized bust of an austere and unforgiving Führer. The court was presided over by Roland Freisler, who excelled at humiliating and intimidating the manacled prisoners before him. They had been stripped of their uniforms and were required to appear in old, shabby clothes without tie or belt. Their treatment at Gestapo HQ was usually evident from their bearing and gait. Little evidence was presented in court by the prosecution and nothing was usually said by the defence. The prisoners' presence in the dock was all the evidence of guilt that was required. They were not permitted to speak and to ensure their compliance they had been reminded that their friends and family were under SS supervision. Each day the proceedings were filmed and the footage was later watched and enjoyed by Hitler. In the first five days of August, Freisler processed 24 senior officers and came to the same conclusion in every case.

Victims and survivors

Statistics relating to the purge are difficult to establish. There were countless deaths in Nazi camps and prisons during the last nine months of the war that might or might not have been connected to Stauffenberg's plot. Conservative estimates suggest that around 7,000 'suspects' were arrested and just under

5,000 of those were executed. Persistent conspirators who were killed included Admiral Canaris and Hans Oster, who were hanged together on 9 April 1945 at Flossenbürg concentration camp. They died in the good company of Pastor Dietrich Bonhöffer. The dithering General Stieff had suffered the same fate at Plötzensee Prison on the previous day. From diaries and other papers found at his home by the SS, the moral influence and encouragement that the lawyer Hans von Dohnányi had offered to many of the conspirators had become clear. He was rewarded with the privilege of being hung by an especially thin cord, so as to prolong his agony on the gallows. The discovery of General Witzleben's involvement in several plots over the years disappointed Hitler. He had liked Witzleben and had considered him a friend. As a result, the general was also hung on a thin hemp cord, but in his case he was also suspended from a meat hook. General Fromm's ploy of killing Stauffenberg immediately to emphasize his loyalty to Hitler won him a generous dispensation from the People's Court. Rather than a traitor's death by hanging, he was awarded an officer's death by firing squad.

As the SS and the Gestapo examined documents that went back to plots in the late 1930s, they gradually discovered the ways in which Fritz-Dietlof von der Schulenberg had strengthened links between isolated plotters and encouraged them to co-operate. He had also drawn up many of the new regulations in the fake Valkyrie plan. An aristocrat, a lawyer and a courageous man with a sense of humour, he was one of the few of the accused who spoke in the *Volksgerichtshof*. Judge Freisler had referred to him as 'the scoundrel Schulenberg' throughout his trial. When Freisler absent-mindedly addressed him by his correct title of Graf or Count, he responded: 'Scoundrel Schulenberg, please.' For that moment of impudent resistance, Freisler ordered that he be hanged that same afternoon.

Suicides, survivors and some tidying up

The post-Stauffenberg purge seems to have jogged the memory of Himmler's operatives about various episodes from Nazi history that had never been properly concluded. Several names from the past were suddenly back on Himmler's agenda. Josef 'Beppo' Römer had gone into the Nazi prison system in 1934 and appears to have been almost forgotten about. Now he was certainly remembered and there seemed to be no further reason to keep him alive. He was executed at Brandenburg-Görden Prison near Berlin in September 1944. Similarly, the beer hall bomber Georg Elser had outlived his usefulness, if he ever really had any. By this late stage in the war, it was obvious that there would never be a show trial of the British agents at the centre of the Venlo incident, so there would be no need for Elser to serve as a witness. After five years in Dachau, an order for his immediate execution signed by Hitler arrived on the camp commander's desk. On 9 April 1945 Elser was shot and his body was immediately thrown into the concentration camp's crematorium.

Several prominent plotters didn't give Hitler or Himmler the opportunity of destroying them. They knew too much about the extent to which a conspiratorial atmosphere had spread through the Wehrmacht in the last two years of the war. And they also knew that they would be singled out for special attention by the Gestapo's interrogators. Their own lives were forfeit but they might be able to save the lives of others. Field Marshal von Kluge had played no part in the 20 July plot but he knew too much about the oppositionists that served in his ranks. Recalled to Berlin for a special meeting with Hitler, Kluge read the message correctly and killed himself using potassium cyanide on 19 August 1944. General Ludwig Beck was even more compromised than Kluge. He had resigned as Chief of Staff at Army High Command in 1938 after many disagreements with Hitler and in retirement he had maintained contact with oppositionist officers. Beck had even been talked about as a suitable interim Chancellor in a provisional government, if Operation Valkyrie was successful. Taken into custody the day after the explosion at Rastenburg, Beck attempted to shoot himself in the head but made a poor job of it. He lingered on for a while until an armed sergeant was found to put him out of his misery.

Major General Henning von Tresckow did not even wait for the summons by the authorities. The moment he learned that Hitler had survived Stauffenberg's bomb he knew that he was a dead man. However, he did not want his death to look like a common suicide so he chose to die in action. During a convenient partisan attack on 21 July 1944 he held a grenade to his throat and pulled the pin. His family gave him an honourable burial on the family estate in Brandenburg. Later in the year, when his role as one of the most determined opponents of Nazism was better understood, the SS dug him up and tossed his remains into the crematorium pits at Sachsenhausen concentration camp.

There were survivors of the purge: Breitenbuch, Gersdorff, Fabian von Schlabrendorff and Axel von dem Bussche were among the lucky ones whose names were not spattered out in the Gestapo torture chamber. All survived the war and lived to pass on their account of the officers of the Wehrmacht who valued their honour more than obedience to Hitler.

At the height of his power in 1938, Hitler felt invincible and invulnerable to attack. Seven momentous years later, having led Germany to defeat and destruction, Hitler succeeded in ending his own life where dozens of plotters and would-be assassins had failed.

The last bullet

From his first days in Bavarian politics in 1920 to the last days of his Empire in 1945, Hitler had been the target of dozens of plotters, many of them unknown. Some had hoped to kill him with poison, most had relied on bullets and bombs. The majority of his early assailants were civilians, motivated by their politics or by their faith and moral feelings to do away with a man they despised. In the last phase of his life, the men who planned to kill him were nearly all professional soldiers, but all had failed. It is little wonder that he believed that he enjoyed a special, invincible destiny. For Germany, the inability of the plotters to do away with him led to the disaster of 1945. Millions died in the nine months between the explosion of Stauffenberg's bomb and Germany's inevitable surrender on 7 May. Hitler clung on through those last futile months of war, his Reich shrinking, his world reduced to little more than a fetid-smelling concrete bomb shelter. Even then he believed in his destiny, hoping that divine Providence would furnish him with a miracle: a new game-changing weapon, a relief army, the death of Roosevelt or better still the sudden death of the drunken warmonger Churchill. Even with the Red Army encircling his capital city, Hitler refused to remove his piece from the chessboard. It was perhaps only the news of Mussolini's naked and battered body hanging like meat in a Milanese street that convinced him there was a better way to end the game. As he looked at the corpse of his wife on the couch beside him, he lifted the Walter PPK to his head and fired a shot that even he could not evade.

Index